'A gem of a book, one that pedagogically
on Black history in schools. A must for
positively interrupt and change their own
justice to hidden histories in general an

Johan Wassermann, Professor oi _____ _____,
University of Pretoria

'This engaging and timely book provides classroom teachers with
essential knowledge and powerful examples of imaginative ways to
implement historical enquires in their classrooms, enabling students to
think creatively and deeply about the ways in which history is constructed
and reconstructed within different social, political, and economic
contexts. The authors also describe ways in which teachers can help
students to construct counter-narratives, challenging master narratives
that marginalize victimized racial and ethnic groups. This innovative,
informative, and needed book deserves a wide and attentive audience.'

**James A. Banks, Kerry and Linda Killinger Endowed Chair in
Diversity Studies, and Director, Center for Multicultural Education,
University of Washington**

'Mohamud and Whitburn present a rationale for teaching fascinating,
important and carefully researched content that is frequently neglected in
the history classroom. They also explore complex questions surrounding
how teachers might select such content. Clear, practical suggestions for
resources and coherent lesson sequences make this a useful guide for any
history department seeking to examine and improve the breadth and
scope of historical knowledge it currently teaches. As a trainer of history
teachers, I am particularly impressed by the thoroughness and winning
detail with which the book builds teachers' knowledge and the care taken
to suggest analytic angles from which students might consider it.'

Dr Christine Counsell, Faculty of Education, University of Cambridge

Doing Justice to History

We dedicate this book to
Amari Chimara and Asia Sheikh Mohamud

Doing Justice to History
Transforming Black history in secondary schools

Abdul Mohamud and Robin Whitburn

 is an imprint of

First published in 2016 by the UCL Institute of Education Press, 20 Bedford Way, London WC1H 0AL

ioepress.co.uk

©2016 Abdul Mohamud and Robin Whitburn

British Library Cataloguing in Publication Data:
A catalogue record for this publication is available from the British Library

ISBNs
978-1-85856-552-1 (paperback)
978-1-85856-772-3 (PDF eBook)
978-1-85856-773-0 (ePub eBook)
978-1-85856-774-7 (Kindle eBook)

Every effort has been made to trace copyright holders and to obtain their permission for the use of copyright material. The publisher apologizes for any errors or omissions and would be grateful if notified of any corrections that should be incorporated in future reprints or editions of this book.

The opinions expressed in this publication are those of the author and do not necessarily reflect the views of the Institute of Education, University of London.

Typeset by Quadrant Infotech (India) Pvt Ltd
Printed by CPI Group (UK) Ltd, Croydon, CR0 4YY

Cover image: detail from *Dawn of Hope* by Colleen Hamer. Reproduced by kind permission of the artist.

Contents

List of figures and tables

Acknowledgements

We have been blessed to have friends and colleagues who have supported us throughout our work on *Doing Justice to History*, and we would like to thank particularly André Burton, Anthony Chimara, Robert Fitzgerald, Anthony Jackson, Alison Kitson and Sharon Yemoh, who talked with us passionately about the ideas we cared about and wanted to share with others, and also read sections of the book and offered their thoughts on different chapters. Thank you so much for your encouragement and wise counsel.

Our three fellow contributors to the book, Michelle Hussain, Martin Spafford and Jenice View, have shone light on dynamic and vital work that is going on in schools in both the UK and US, and have been a source of inspiration for us as we strive to transform Black history education. Thank you for your stimulating contributions and gracious patience with our organization and deadlines.

It has been our privilege to work in a number of London schools over the last few years, piloting the historical enquiries that appear in this book. The students and teachers in those schools have constantly inspired us to develop our work in new ways, and many of their thoughts and ideas appear in the book. We would like to particularly thank Jamie Abbott, Eddie Crust, Katie Dennis, Steven Harlow, Zara Hassan, Pablo Hinojo, Rebecca Hulme, Charlotte Kourreas, Catherine Lunn and Tim Spafford for their creative collaborations with us on our enquiries.

We have also had formative discussions with colleagues at University College London's Institute of Education (IOE), and our teachers over many years, and thank them for their inspiration and advice, particularly Katharine Burn, Arthur Chapman, Alex Moore, Philip Philippou, David Sim, Victoria Showunmi and Paddy Walsh.

Students have always been the most powerful source of inspiration to us, and we particularly thank Daniel Brobby, Devanté Jackson, Mongiwa Khumalo and Jordan Morris for always being prepared to meet and talk about history and education throughout the past five years. We thank all the students in London schools who have joined us in researching and thinking about history education, and particularly those at Hampstead School, St Mary's Hendon and Westminster City School.

Our work in Black history has taken us to South Africa and the wonderful Maritzburg Christian School three times since 2012, and we are so grateful to the headteacher, Eugene Burger, and his amazing school community for the *ubuntu* and friendship that has inspired our work on South African history and historical enquiry in general. Many thanks to Kalma Savage and all the history classes we taught. A very special thank you to Colleen Hamer for her wonderful artwork, which became our front cover.

We have also been welcomed in the US and had the privilege of speaking at the Citadel in Charleston, South Carolina. Thank you so much to Renee Jefferson and all our friends there, for their magnificent Southern hospitality and interest in our work. Thanks also to Yolanda Sealey-Ruiz for her welcome to New York, and to Elaine Hall and Cynthia Patterson-Lewis for their hospitality at the Martin Luther King Center in Atlanta.

Thanks to Gillian Klein and the team at Trentham Books/UCL-IOE Press for their patience, guidance and encouragement in our first book project.

Finally, we thank our friends and families, who have shared the challenges and demands of this work and have been nothing but supportive and considerate throughout. Amari Chimara, Robin's godson, assured us that merely writing a book does not make us wise – he says we have to retire before we can claim that! We hope our book has the beginnings of wisdom nonetheless, but we acknowledge its shortcomings, which are fully our responsibility. Amari says we are still reckless before we retire, so we hope to enjoy that for some time to come!

About the authors and contributors

Michelle Hussain is Head of Humanities at Willowfield School in Walthamstow, London, and a Lead Practitioner in History. She is a Lead Mentor for the Postgraduate Certificate in Education (PGCE) programme in secondary history education at the UCL Institute of Education. A History graduate of Queen Mary's, London University, Michelle's postgraduate studies are in curriculum studies and history education. Michelle and Robin worked for over ten years together at St Mary's High School in Hendon, where they pioneered innovative work in Black history through the curriculum and the annual History of Black Origin (HYBO) celebrations.

Abdul Mohamud is a Senior Teaching Fellow at the UCL Institute of Education, tutoring trainee history teachers. He is a member of the Historical Association's Secondary Committee, and has spoken at educational conferences in Chicago, Charleston, London, Bristol, Leeds and Manchester. A history graduate of Goldsmith's College, London University, Abdul's postgraduate studies are in history education and leadership. He has taught a wide range of courses for students from 11 to 18 in History, Religious Studies and Sociology. Abdul is of Somali heritage and has eight years' experience of working with young people from diverse ethnic backgrounds. Abdul founded Justice to History with Robin as an organization to help teachers and students explore relevant, and often neglected, diverse histories.

Martin Spafford has spent over 40 years working with young people in London, South Yorkshire, Southern Africa and Egypt. He has recently retired after 23 years of teaching history at George Mitchell School in Waltham Forest, where he and his students explored – through a range of projects – how a deeper understanding of the past can inform and inspire our understanding of ourselves. He continues – working with Journey to Justice and Facing History and Ourselves – to develop these ideas with young people. Through the Black and Asian Studies Association he is working with the exam board OCR on the development of GCSE units

on the history of migration to Britain and remains deeply involved with the
Schools History Project.

Jenice L. View is an Associate Professor in the Graduate School of
Education at George Mason University. She holds degrees from Syracuse
University, Princeton University and the Union Institute and University. Her
scholarship focuses on the critical teaching and learning of history, critical
pedagogy in teacher professional development and how the learning of
history impacts upon youth voice and civic engagement. She has created a
graduate certificate programme at George Mason called Learning Historic
Places with Diverse Populations. Her work in the state of Mississippi to
teach the Civil Rights Movement has impacted upon teachers and students
in 14 schools. She is creator and host of 'Urban Education: Issues and
Solutions', an award-winning cable television programme with GMU-TV.

Robin Whitburn is a Lecturer in History Education at the UCL
Institute of Education. He is a Quality Mark Assessor for the Historical
Association, and has spoken at educational conferences in Beijing,
Vancouver, Chicago, Charleston, London, Bristol, Leeds and Manchester.
A history graduate of the London School of Economics, Robin's doctoral
thesis was on successful pedagogy with African–Caribbean male students
in secondary school. He has 30 years' experience in teaching history,
economics and mathematics in secondary education, and has taught on
teacher training and other graduate courses for history educators for the
last five years. Robin is a co-director, with Abdul, of Justice to History.

Introduction

> '...the past is not simply prologue; it is indelibly part of our collective destiny'.
>
> (Manning Marable, *Living Black History*, 2006)

This book has been inspired by teachers who have striven to challenge the absence of Black history in the curriculum by teaching hidden histories in their own classrooms, and by resolute activists who campaigned for justice for Black history. Our own journey in writing this book owes a great debt to their tireless efforts. In our work with young people we have been driven by the conviction that Black history plays an active role in all our lives and that it is our duty to explore it with them.

Over a period of five years we taught all the historical enquiries presented in this book in secondary schools in London and South Africa. Our interactions with students convinced us of the unique potential of such culturally relevant historical enquiries to develop ideas of identity and meaning for young people in an increasingly challenging and complex world. We hope teachers will find this book gives them the knowledge and confidence to engage with their students in dialogic learning through these enquiries. Teachers have been held back from tackling the ambitious demands of Black history by an absence of both knowledge and confidence, and this book seeks to help overcome such barriers. We hope to support our colleagues in this challenge.

Our strong belief in the power of history education to further social justice in schools and universities has encouraged us to help teachers transform their practice and revolutionize their curricula. Through their teachers' efforts in the field of Black history, school students can take greater ownership of their learning of history and develop both a greater sense of their ability to function as co-creators of knowledge and the assurance to take that knowledge beyond the classroom. Throughout the lessons and research interviews considered in this book we have been reminded of the insight and creativity of young people, who continue to inspire our own learning as we develop our work. We embark on this exploration of Black history with all those fellow teachers and students in our thoughts, and invite you to share our ambition of 'doing justice to history'.

Chapter 1

Pugilists, diggers and choreographers

Doing justice to history is the ambition of all good history teachers. This book aims to support teachers in teaching Black history by combining relevant knowledge with a pedagogy rooted in a spirit of enquiry that intrigues and engages students. Chapters 2 to 7 describe the enquiries we developed to teach six narratives of Black history, and the transformational impact the approach we developed has had on the students and their teachers.

This introductory chapter looks at the barriers and challenges to teaching Black history in a meaningful way in secondary schools and describes how to overcome them. The approach we have used can best be explained using three metaphors: doing justice to Black history is achieved by pugilists, diggers and choreographers. The pugilists fight for greater justice in history education and for inclusive, diverse curricula in schools; the diggers work as historians to uncover the sources needed to develop full and inclusive historical understandings; and the choreographers bring histories into the learning theatres: school classrooms.

Policy makers in education have long deemed Black history undeserving of the respect and reverence afforded to traditionally taught history, so we need pugilists to take up the struggle against the master narratives in history education and historical scholarship that exclude the histories of people from the African continent and the African diaspora over the past two millennia. But the roles of the diggers and choreographers are equally essential.

The diggers devote themselves to researching and collecting important stories that have the power to challenge conventional thinking about Black history: they reveal its diversity, its intrigues and the inevitable accompanying narratives of its obscuration. Diggers trawl archives and libraries for new material on people and events that have been largely ignored in the mainstream narratives. Teachers can do some of the digging themselves, but with the limitations of time they often rely on the work of others, particularly through online communities. Moreover, the neglected histories we want to unearth are rarely the stuff of university history programmes. There are few undergraduate or even postgraduate courses in

British universities where students can study Black British history, although there are some beacons of hope. The Black and Asian Studies Association (BASA) is a pioneering organization that has for decades helped to bring together diggers who are working in the UK. The appointment of Hakim Adi, one of BASA's founders, as professor of the history of Africa and the African diaspora at the University of Chichester in 2014–15 was a major breakthrough for Black history in British universities. The opening of the Black Cultural Archives (BCA, 2014) in South London in 2014 is another.

The United States has a much longer tradition of scholarly work in the field of Black history, although this has been seen almost exclusively in terms of African-American history. Since Carter G. Woodson launched the *Journal of Negro History* (now the *Journal of African American History*) in 1916, and initiated the first Negro History Week (now Black History Month) in 1926, scholarship on African-American history has been encouraged in a number of American universities. Yet even in the US, pugilists and diggers cannot guarantee the position of their subject in the discourses of American history across schools and colleges. As a result, African-American young people, indeed all American students, are given an impoverished curriculum in the field of history (Grant, 2011).

The matter of choreography brings us to the classroom of the history teacher. Some teachers remain content to be 'embroiderers' (Whitman, 2015), merely embellishing the surface of historical narratives. They may occasionally *mention* figures of Black history, but do not strive to explore the complex fibres of authentic historical research. Teacher-choreographers, on the other hand, are ambitious. History teachers are already choreographing the work of others when they introduce new history into the classroom. It is classroom teachers who gather new subject material, balance its distribution across a sequence of lessons, and elicit meaning from it for their students. Good teachers encourage their students to express themselves through the medium of learning in historical enquiries.

A good deal of the choreographer's work is done in advance of the lessons, by carefully planning the questions and stimulus material. But our choreographers also take part in the dance. They model the thinking and learning processes students will engage in, and guide them in undertaking independent reasoning and research (Mohamud and Whitburn, 2014). The history teachers who lead the way in striving to do justice to Black history will be in the vanguard of the operation to develop high-quality historical thinking in the enquiry, without diminishing the independent thinking they demand of their students.

However, being an accomplished choreographer is rarely enough for a teacher to bring innovative Black history to a school. All too often it is a challenge for the one teacher to convince their departmental colleagues that including Black history could transform the curriculum. And it is even more of a struggle when senior leaders in school question efforts to change the dominant discourse of history education. Robin once told a senior school leader about his plans to introduce Black history into a rather moribund school curriculum after the 1991 reforms, and was told, 'All right, but not too much of it!' He was fortunately in a position to navigate the political channels so the choreography could continue.

A colleague of ours was less successful when she attempted to bring one of our Black history enquiries into the boys' comprehensive school where she had recently started her career. Her proposed innovation secured initial approval, but then fell victim to senior leadership politics and was prohibited for two years. She was stunned by the cavalier treatment she received and the way she saw race emerge in curriculum policy-making in this ethnically diverse school. Although totally unprepared for the pugilist role, she rapidly realized that pugilism would be needed alongside all her choreography skills if she were ever to succeed in doing justice to Black history in her school.

Teachers must be prepared to take on any or all of the roles of choreographer, digger and pugilist when they undertake to transform Black history in a school. They must understand the way in which each role functions in the transformation. Pugilists, diggers and choreographers have to unite and together strengthen their impact in this ever uphill campaign. We encourage them to unite in a 'troika', a group of three acting in unison to exert optimal influence (Dictionary.com, n.d.). This book explains how these roles have furthered our work in London schools.

Justice, race and history

We believe that doing justice to history differs from doing justice to most other academic disciplines and school subjects because of its moral as well as intellectual dimension. Teachers do justice to all subject areas and studies by keeping to the principles and values of that area of knowledge and thought. But history teachers are deeply involved in issues of justice. Studying history involves making connections with the moral conditions of past times, and with the works and worlds of historians who have made claims about those times. From its inception in 1991 the English National Curriculum for History tended to avoid such responsibilities (QCA, 2007), preferring to keep to cognitive concepts such as causation, change and continuity, and chronological understanding. The Canadian Historical Thinking project, by contrast, adds a vital element alongside the cognitive foundations in its 'Big Six' ideas concerning the 'Ethical Dimensions of History' (Seixas and Morton, 2013). Seixas and his team pioneered the inclusion of Aboriginal histories, for instance, and Canadian school curricula confront longstanding issues of social justice and fairness. It is not only Canada that should feature injustice in its history curricula; there have been major injustices in the pasts of other Western societies, and major injustices, too, in the way historians have interpreted the past.

We share Michael Apple's preference for a bold commitment to social justice that shuns notions of 'neutrality' (Apple, 2004), and are guided by the approach of Amartya Sen, who considers the righting of injustices to be at the heart of the matter (Sen, 2010). We don't begin with a *tabula rasa* and set out the ideal secondary history curriculum; instead we suggest a way of challenging the serious omissions and distortions in historical narratives that have been used to support popular and, in particular, racist approaches. Established master narratives glorify the stories of Westerners and construct notions of race that confine others to levels of inferiority (Willinsky, 1998). White hegemony ignores the histories of people outside the white world, especially Africa and its diaspora.

Manning Marable discusses the demands of doing justice to Black history in terms of 'authentic' history:

> By 'authentic' I mean a historical narrative in which blacks themselves are the principal actors, and that the story is told and explained largely from their own vantage point. The authentic narrative rejects out of hand the inferiority – biological, genetic, or cultural – of people of African descent to any other branches of the human family.
>
> (Marable, 2006: 21)

Such authenticity has not been a typical feature of the way Black history is treated in our schools. Master narratives are often presented didactically, and can be fashioned as 'facts' that need to be learned to earn a place in that society by acquiring what Hirsch (1988) terms 'cultural literacy'. The students have no voice. Teachers are shackled to the enormous volume of enshrined information that needs to be covered, leaving no room for other ideas to flourish. Grant and Gradwell's work on ambitious history teachers in New York state relates the efforts by one history teacher in a highly successful school to introduce a more authentic approach to African history. He wrote: 'When I talked to some teachers about what the kids really needed to know about Africa, the first answer I got was "Nothing"' (Grant and Gradwell, 2010: 26). The hegemonic assertion of white Western history usually operates more subtly than this.

Opponents of Black history and multicultural education have argued that teaching Black history is mostly a matter of mythology and lacks validity. Their denials are entangled with their conceptions of race. Racism is not simply a matter of 'human nature', it is a historical phenomenon that developed during the early modern period, partly to justify white domination of darker-skinned peoples through slavery. It is a historical feature with particular causal influences, which does not therefore have to be part of the human condition (Saxton, 1990). Racism is not just prejudice or discrimination; it is about the systematic domination of particular peoples by other groups aspiring to hegemony. The development of the ideas of race and racism in the modern world is charted through the historical enquiries developed in this book. These ideas developed in fifteenth-century Europe from perceptions of social reality and of the domination of white races over Africans (Saxton, 1990). This fleeting social reality expanded into a rationalization and a means of perpetuating the terms of superiority.

We encounter constructions of race in varied circumstances. Children from minority ethnic backgrounds still encounter negative experiences to do with race that could potentially damage their sense of self-worth. They can be made to feel they have to 'be responsible for [their] body, [their] race, [their] ancestors', as Frantz Fanon declared (quoted in Holt, 1995: 2). Children need the opportunity to explore their racial identities in a positive and constructive environment. Thomas Holt wrote about the 'burden of our history-making' in challenging the 'everydayness' of racism in society and about the need to provide counter-stories to the singular narratives that seem to emerge so easily from national histories (Holt, 1995). The present book seeks to take up that burden.

Black history in English schools

Although the British master narrative founded on the Whig interpretation of the past has been critiqued for decades, it remains a major barrier to the learning of Black history. The Whig interpretation presents English history as the inexorable unfolding of the triumphant progressive forces of Protestantism, parliamentary democracy and monarchy across the centuries, and assumes the positive influence of British ideals and actions around the world. As in the debates over revisions to the National Curriculum for history in England in 2013, supporters of this view argue that the history curriculum must feature an extensive array of the significant moments in

Britain's inexorable rise to greatness, from the Norman conquest through Magna Carta, the Reformation, the civil war, the industrial revolution and up to the British Empire. This leaves no room for anything else. When people become weary of the complexities of diversity, the established view is a popular option. But if history is reduced to grand historical narratives, Black history is relegated to an isolated corner of the curriculum. Consequently, the justification for its inclusion needs to be clear and resolute and history teachers must stand with the pugilists.

Pioneering work in teaching Black history began in the US early in the twentieth century, but in the UK its influence only really began to be felt in the 1980s. During this decade the Inner London Education Authority led the production of anti-racist curricula that included the history of peoples of Africa and the diaspora (Brandt, 1986), and the first UK Black History Month was celebrated in London in 1987. Although this event featured in a number of schools in metropolitan areas, it was not a mainstream development.

So when schools in England were obliged in 1991 to follow a National Curriculum in the early years of secondary education (a period termed Key Stage 3) (Department for Education and Science, 1991), the compulsory units focused on the chronological narrative of British history with no reference to the participation of Black people. There was an optional unit entitled 'Black Peoples of the Americas' that could be chosen as the one 'world history unit' schools were required to teach, but this pioneering curriculum began with the account of Black people as slaves in the transatlantic trade of the early modern world, wholly omitting the history of the ancient and medieval civilizations of Africa. Although this did not match the approach of the local authority anti-racist projects, the course outline became the foundation of a number of textbooks for secondary schools, some of which are still in print in their original form (e.g. Smith, 1992).

Black history in English schools has generally remained a narrative of victims who emerged out of primitive contexts to face lives of struggle. Schools did not have actively to promote the ideas of Hegel or Trevor-Roper, or support the principles of the Hamitic myth, in order to contribute to negative stereotypes of Black people; their coverage of slavery was enough to maintain the folk culture in playgrounds and wider community arenas that kept Black people out of the realms of nation-building and socio-economic advancement.

Pioneering work did persist after 1991 (e.g. Grosvenor, 1999; Lyndon, 2006), and a few key Black British individuals, like Mary Seacole and Olaudah Equiano, joined Martin Luther King and Nelson Mandela as worthy of mention in history lessons. However, they often served as token figures rather than representing a more just overall approach to the exploration of historical narratives. The danger is that the few selected aspects of Black history that are included in the school curriculum might themselves form a minor established narrative. This can be seen in the way the American Civil Rights Movement history is often taught in English schools, with Martin Luther King in his non-violent resistance triumphing over the terrors of violent Black rebellion urged by Malcolm X. The complexities of both men's positions are ignored, as is the significance of other Black leaders on both sides of the Atlantic. To illustrate this, Chapter 4 takes Robert F. Williams as the protagonist of the enquiry on the Civil Rights Movement. Williams, who began as a leader in his local branch of the National Association for the Advancement of Colored People (the NAACP) (renowned as an organization that worked for legal and constitutional change in civil rights) and became a staunch defender of armed self-defence against the Ku Klux Klan, would merit much attention if British teachers had a broader knowledge of American history.

In British history curricula, many significant figures are equally neglected. Take, for example, Paul Stephenson, a leader in the Bristol Bus Boycott of 1963, a struggle that merits a place in English historical enquiries as much as do the heroes of the Montgomery affair seven years earlier. Doing justice to Black history in schools demands not only a secure position for the field, but also a vibrant exploration of neglected histories, calling upon history teachers to become diggers or to establish strong connections with diggers elsewhere. Black history is likely to remain contested for decades to come and will have to be treated as a distinct field if its position is to be established and defended. But the field can be richly populated.

Defining Black history

Educators have descriptive labels for the term 'history'. Some of them signify functional aspects of the societies described, such as 'political, economic or religious' history, while others pinpoint the socio-geographic scope of the studies, usually on the basis of the nation-state, giving us English, British, Russian or Indian history. In multicultural nations like the UK or US there are diverse histories associated with their many peoples. The connection between doing justice to history and a focus on Black history goes beyond the inclusion of one more particular kind of history in the curriculum. We believe that Black history merits inclusion in a potentially crowded curriculum on its own distinctive basis.

There is already a precedent for such 'exceptionalism' in doing justice to history. The unique programme of the Nazis to systematically wipe out the entire Jewish population of the world is accepted as giving the Holocaust an exceptional imperative in the school curriculum; other genocides are often included alongside the history of the Holocaust, but the latter's primacy is unassailable. Black history similarly has uniqueness because of the systematic attempt by the Western world to eradicate the centuries-old history of the Black peoples of Africa.

Our focus on teaching Black history in schools is founded on this political and historiographical issue, as well as the socio-cultural aspects of our multicultural nation; our students should learn an authentic and richly researched history of African peoples that will help to dispel the myths of the 'Dark Continent' that Hegel and others have promoted since the eighteenth century. In his philosophy of history lectures, delivered in Germany in the 1820s, Hegel stated: 'What we properly understand by Africa is the Unhistorical, Undeveloped Spirit ... It is no historical part of the world; it has no movement or development to exhibit' (quoted in Willinsky, 1998: 118). The injustice of that myth has a negative impact not only on the Black students in our schools, but also on the non-Black students whose understanding is compromised if they accept that myth.

Historical enquiries

Doing justice to history is centred on the well-formed judgements of teachers about the curriculum that students should encounter, but also considers the way in which they learn best about the past and its interpretations. We should not pursue greater diversity in the school curriculum without also seeking to develop the best pedagogy. Explicit throughout this book is the idea of teaching history in secondary schools by means of an enquiry: a sequence of around seven lessons that focuses on one intriguing and demanding enquiry question. This approach requires students to work with the processes and concepts of the discipline of history itself so as to construct answers to that question (Riley, 2000).

The beginning of the enquiry process should be, as John Dewey (1933) emphasized, the establishment of a 'felt difficulty' for those who undertake the enquiry (Barton and Levstik, 2004). This approach emphasizes the importance of the question at the heart of the sequence of lessons. Such an approach calls for the enquiries to be connected to issues and ideas that matter to the students, or for the creation of an intrigue that builds new connections for them. As Barton and Levstik point out, it is imperative that historical thinking and learning go beyond the conceptual procedures recommended by those who emphasize the centrality of teaching history as a discipline; they found that the 'felt difficulty' is 'often missing in history classrooms both in the United States and elsewhere' (Barton and Levstik, 2004: 198).

Such an enquiry would certainly not compromise the rigour of the learning for the sake of holding students' interest. Powerful enquiry-based learning in history has to incorporate the rigorous historical thinking that is rooted in the integration of key, well-established 'second-order' concepts, including causation, continuity and change. We want to integrate *procedural* justice with other aspects of doing justice to Black history, so we have worked with questions that range across a number of second-order concepts. When Black history emerged as a valuable component of the Black Studies movement in American education in the early 1970s, pioneering educator and activist for civil rights and equality James Banks stressed the importance of a rigorous disciplinary approach to history in the new curriculum:

> [T]he main goal of Black history should be the same as the goal of the social studies program: to help students develop the ability to make sound decisions so that they can resolve personal problems and shape public policy by participating in intelligent social action. Higher-level interdisciplinary knowledge, social science inquiry, and value inquiry are necessary for sound decision-making.
>
> (Banks, 2006: 27)

Banks warned that without this disciplinary stance and a new pedagogical approach from teachers, 'Black history will become just another fleeting fad.' Where there is no available curriculum support from local authorities or other providers, Black History Month is unlikely to be handled well in schools. Too many schools in Britain labour to mark the occasion simply with a display featuring prominent figures such as Nelson Mandela and Martin Luther King. These individuals' stories are generally presented as exclusively celebratory and unproblematic. King's radical condemnation of both capitalism and war in the late 1960s is rarely considered, nor is Mandela's choice concerning direct action tactics of sabotage debated (we explore the place of these figures and their politics in history in chapters 4 and 5). The process of enquiry can overcome superficial celebration and encourage school students to engage in meaningful historical debate by exploring historical sources and interpretations.

Dialogue, discovery and the enquiry approach

As they construct historical enquiries, teachers establish an engaging learning process in which students can develop independent approaches while remaining connected to a collective educational venture. Their independent learning does not isolate them from the teacher or their fellow students. The independence lies in their response to the enquiry, in asking further questions and in selecting evidence and ideas to bring to the enquiry. The process requires dialogue with classmates – another key feature of the historical enquiry. We work in accordance with Nicholas Burbules's definition of dialogue; he distinguishes clearly between dialogue and other forms of talk that might happen in or outside the classroom, such as chatting and arguing:

> Dialogue is an activity directed toward discovery and new understanding, which stands to improve the knowledge, insight, or sensitivity of its participants … In some cases, a dialogue might have an intended goal, such as answering a specific question or communicating an already-formulated insight.
>
> (Burbules, 1993: 8)

The enquiry process sets the students on individual journeys of discovery as they unravel and interpret the enquiry question for themselves. But they do so as part of a class, led by the teacher, and their voice expresses not only their perspective on the enquiry at a particular point but also their own personal identity. Participation in the dialogue allows for the co-agency that the Learning Without Limits project team found to be so vital to transformative learning when they researched successful mixed-ability teaching (Hart *et al.*, 2004), and that French philosopher Michel de Montaigne advocated in the sixteenth century:

> I do not want the tutor to be the only one to choose topics or to do all the talking: when the boy's turn comes let the tutor listen to his [*sic*] pupil talking. Socrates and then Archesilaus used to make their pupils speak first; they spoke afterwards. For those who want to learn, the obstacle can often be the authority of those who teach.
>
> (Montaigne, 2004: 43)

There is a sense of shared influence in the learning process here, though without requiring an equalization of authority between teacher and student.

The enquiry process gives the students a voice, inviting them to participate in the investigation of a significant question.

Barton and Levstik highlighted another social effect of the enquiry process: it takes away the advantage for the students in a traditional classroom who had already amassed knowledge about the topic, thus making for greater equality in the classroom. These authors maintain that in the enquiry process, 'all students will be positioned to develop a more complete and nuanced understanding of history, and that this understanding may be more equitably distributed' (Barton and Levstik, 2004: 190). As a redistributive process, this can have both positive and negative effects. We observed this in one of the Year 8 classes that studied our British Somali history enquiry (see Chapter 7). Before the enquiry, the highest-achieving student, 13-year-old Marcus, displayed a sophisticated knowledge of history in the research group but was muted in his response to the enquiry lessons, and was clearly uncomfortable in the post-enquiry discussion. In the lessons he had been eclipsed by students who had shown little enthusiasm for learning history at first, but who then relished the validation of their own knowledge construction that the enquiry problem and resources enabled. One of these students, Parvez, remarked on the difference learning through enquiry had made to him:

> I like that there's different, not opinions, but answers that you can state, like this happened; there's different things. We saw two different people, and it shows that, how different Somalis, like, act in different circumstances ... I like where there's different answers, and it's good for my mind to have a challenge.
>
> When we used to do [history] with our regular teacher, it's way different, because that was more closed, and we get told the answer, and we have to know it, but here we don't know the answer, we just like make up our opinion and structure our answer.
>
> (Parvez, Year 8 student)

Marcus, on the other hand, appeared overwhelmed by this openness, but his alienation was probably temporary; in time he would almost certainly have channelled his undoubted intellectual ability into the new mode of learning. For Parvez, however, the new process represented a timely reprieve from unjust confinement in a mode of learning he would always struggle with.

What you will find in this book

Doing justice to Black history is a call to action rather than the proclamation of an imminent goal. The injustices of the past and the interpretations of it, which we call 'history', are so complex and so embedded in social and personal psyches, to say nothing of school texts and syllabuses, that the struggles for Black history are unlikely to end. We see doing justice to Black history not as a final product but as a process that invites teachers and other supporters to keep mounting challenges in the years ahead.

In this book we present six historical enquiries into different areas of Black history that teachers can incorporate into their syllabuses and schemes of learning. Each chapter explores the roles of pugilist, digger and choreographer for the teacher who wants to develop this enquiry from scratch in their school. The stories that form the core of the enquiries are not necessarily about the familiar heroes of traditional Black history narratives, where these exist. In finding the basis for transformation, we have chosen stories that present challenges and ambiguities, so that school students can find a culturally relevant history that connects with the complexities of their own lives, rather than a panacea for an existence without race or racism. Often the enquiries *interrupt the psyches* of students and teachers, a key concept we use in this book to account for how someone or something challenges the conventional thinking about a situation in the past and dismantles assumptions made about history (see Chapter 6). Such interruptions challenge students' and teachers' preconceptions about peoples of Africa and the diaspora across the globe.

The first section of each chapter considers aspects of the pugilism relevant to that curricular area, the preconceptions to be challenged and how to transform classroom practice. A section devoted to historical knowledge about the topic follows; this is the result of our own digging into the scholarship of others and is more an analytical essay rather than a comprehensive survey of the field. The next section is the choreographed story, explaining how we planned the historical enquiry at the heart of the chapter. We then include an outline of all the lessons in that enquiry, so it is possible to follow something of the flow of the students' experience in the classroom and to see the pedagogy involved. Further materials concerning the enquiries can be found via the Justice2History website at www.justice2history.org. We finish each chapter with a discussion of transformation within the particular historical field, initial evaluations of the impact of teaching the enquiry in a school and thoughts on how teachers can move forward with this enquiry in their own schools.

The most commonly taught Black history topic in British schools is slavery in the New World of the Americas, so we have placed this chapter first, not because we believe it to be most important, but rather because it is the area of Black school history most taught, and because it is the topic that is most in need of transformation. African history should be the starting point for Black history in the school curriculum. Accordingly, we offer an example in the following chapter. It focuses on the history of Timbuktu, which illustrates the early development of civilization and learning in Africa, through the synthesis of Islam and traditional African culture, in a place that became a byword in Western myths for the remote and inaccessible.

The African American Civil Rights Movement vies with slavery as the most commonly taught Black history topic across the world, so that comes next. Our work eschews the conventional 'Martin and Malcolm' story and approaches civil rights by considering a forgotten character involved in the events of the 1950s and early 1960s: Robert F. Williams, of Monroe, North Carolina. Williams was a controversial figure, and his story presents students with complex and subtle ideas about rights and self-defence, and the interaction of race, gender and class in historical contexts.

A second chapter on African history follows, set centuries after the glory of Timbuktu. Chapter 5 examines recent South African history during apartheid, but takes as its central figure a white man of Afrikaner heritage, Rev Beyers Naudé, rather than Nelson Mandela or the important but neglected PAC leader Robert Sobukwe. Chapters 6 and 7 turn to Black British history, itself a much-neglected area of study. One explores the significance of Black people in Britain across the centuries, with a spotlight on Claudia Jones, a woman from Trinidad who became influential in both the USA and the UK in the mid-twentieth century. The other considers the history of Somali people in Britain. Somalis are often considered to be historically the least significant of Black groups in Britain's history, because they are seen as the most recent arrivals, following the civil war in Somalia in the 1990s. However, our research into the Somali community in Cardiff uncovers an involvement in Britain's story since 1870.

The impact of history education should extend far beyond the classroom. We hope that these enquiries inspire students to want to take home their learning of history with pride, much as they would a special poem from their English lesson, a composition from music or a painting from art. There are many opportunities to be involved in history education beyond the classroom, through public celebrations and exhibitions, and through active citizenship that is rooted in historical understanding and motivation. Our penultimate chapter presents three different stories of such Black history beyond the classroom. Dr Jenice View of George Mason University provides a valuable account of how the African American Civil Rights Movement has been tackled in American history education efforts to 'do justice to history'. There follow two accounts from history educators in London schools who have undertaken outstanding work with their students to extend their history education experience: Martin Spafford discusses two curriculum-based projects that involved his students in east London in developing their own responses to historically inspired contemporary challenges, and Michelle Hussain writes about her North London school's approach to celebrating Black History Month, and about an educational visit to South Africa as part of her senior students' examination course.

The concluding chapter reflects on ways in which teachers and students across schools and colleges might work to transform Black history education in such a way that individuals and communities feel that justice has indeed been achieved. In such attempts at transformation, there has to be unity among those who seek to bring about change and develop understandings. Our book joins the work of those people in the field of history education who are committed to changing the curriculum and pedagogy in schools so that the history of peoples of Africa and the diaspora – 'Black history' – takes its rightful place in the school curriculum.

Despite the worthy efforts of pugilists, diggers and choreographers on both sides of the Atlantic, progress in transforming Black history in school curricula has been slow (Grant, 2011; Boffey, 2014). It is clear that the explanation lies partly in wider social and political frameworks, which manifest the damage caused by institutional racism. So doing justice to Black history is not straightforward. However, activists who want transformation can study one another's work and unite in developing historical enquiries into Black history in secondary schools. We do not offer this work as a catalogue of easy answers, but share with Raymond Williams the prospect of a journey of hope that we can undertake together:

> It is only in a shared belief and insistence that there are practical alternatives that the balance of forces and chances begins to alter. Once the inevitabilities are challenged, we begin gathering our resources for a journey of hope. If there are no easy answers, there are still available and discoverable hard answers, and it is these that we can learn to make and share.
>
> (Williams, quoted in Halpin, 2003: 127)

Chapter 2

Transforming the teaching of the transatlantic slave trade

'Black Peoples of the Americas'

After we completed the enquiries related in Chapters 3 to 7, we reluctantly conceded that we had to do one on slavery – and to put it first. There are two compelling reasons: first, that the slave trade is too often the only topic on Black history that is taught in schools and, second, that it is seldom taught in a way that does justice to history. It is but one episode in Black history, yet the transatlantic slave trade can end up defining the people of the African diaspora.

The growth of far-right groups throughout Britain in the 1970s and 1980s had impelled many educators to act against racism in society through their schools and classrooms (Brandt, 1986). Despite this, the teaching of Black history of any kind was not mandatory in the first National Curriculum in 1991, although Black history could be taught to students aged 11–14 as part of the world history requirement. The 1991 curriculum offered a supplementary unit for the world history option entitled 'Black Peoples of the Americas'. Sadly, this pioneering unit of Black history for English schools totally disregarded African civilizations and polities in the centuries before the Europeans and Arabs arrived, and began with the transatlantic slave trade and European encounters with Africans. The school textbooks (e.g. Smith, 1992) reflected that narrow focus.

In 2007 the revised National Curriculum for history included the transatlantic slave trade and its abolition as a statutory topic (the only other compulsory topic was the Holocaust), partly through the efforts of Culture Minister David Lammy, the African–Caribbean MP for Tottenham (QCA, 2007). Although schools were recommended to preface this compulsory unit with material on early African civilizations, the textbooks and schools' schemes of work generally remained much as before. In our own classrooms, we had always sought to minimize coverage of New World slavery and focus on the early African kingdoms, and then on African resistance to European forces, allocating little more than one lesson to the transatlantic slave trade.

The requirement to teach about slavery and abolition was withdrawn from the revised National Curriculum of 2013, but the topic remains widely taught in schools. Although the enslavement of African people in the Americas was a significant aspect of Black history, to teach only this is to grossly distort school history. So our priority was to develop other enquiries. However, in order for this book to contribute to the transformation of Black history in our schools, a chapter on the slave trade and the Americas seemed inescapable. It was thus with trepidation that we embarked upon the challenge of developing a classroom enquiry that had at its core some of the important issues that have been neglected in school history.

Many of the schemes of work available to schools focus on the economic aspect of the trade. Students might study, for example, the records of the Slave Compensation Commission of 1834, held at the National Archives in London, which list the number of slaves held by each British planter alongside their monetary value. The records are detailed because slaves were assets of high value. They serve as a reminder that even after the political and scientific revolutions of the preceding century, the worth of a human being's life remained equivalent to scrawlings on a promissory note.

Classroom lessons and activities generally restrict the study of slavery to the trade, exemplified by the iconic map depicting the transatlantic triangle. One popular teaching activity even invites students to role-play as economic agents in the triple transactions (the subject of the narrative). Although the economic consequences of the transatlantic slave trade were vital for the development of Western nations' power bases in global history, we wanted rather to focus on socio-political rather than economic matters, and to place the issue of race centre stage. This presents challenges for those teachers who seldom investigate the dynamics of race and oppression. White teachers in multicultural classrooms may find it challenging to work with students descended from slaves (Howard, 2006; Landsman and Lewis, 2011).

People of African descent, like Jewish people, find the story of their forebears' brutal oppression and murder painful, and not a welcome aspect of their racial identity (Traille, 2007; Epstein, 2009). Some teachers attempt to temper the racial element of the trade by placing it within the 'bigger picture' of slavery across millennia, beginning with slavery in ancient times and ending up with 'modern-day slavery'. However, earlier societies that used slave labour, including those in Africa, could be described as 'societies *with* slaves', whereas the plantation economies of the New World of the Americas became 'slave societies', fundamentally defined by the number of slaves, who were identified by their colour. Asserting continuity with earlier societies with slaves can diminish the exceptionalism of New World chattel slavery. Besides, the comparison with modern-day slavery seems unhelpful because contemporary people-trafficking is universally condemned and criminalized by nations across the globe, whereas the transatlantic trade was legal, and indeed the key driver for Western expansion and growth.

To do justice to the teaching of the transatlantic slave trade from Africa to the Americas, it must be prefaced by a history of African civilizations and polities, so as to clearly establish that the Black peoples of the Americas (National Curriculum, 1991) were not wrenched from a continent that had no developed socio-cultural life and little economic promise (see Chapter 3). However, this focus on the continuity of civilized African history has to be followed by an examination of how some African communities were involved in selling African people to the Europeans. This sits uneasily with the warranted narrative of European exploitation and infamy on the West African coast and of the Atlantic crossing. It would be too easy for white Europeans to seize on this detail to exonerate the European traders: 'the Africans did it to themselves'. African complicity in New World Slavery has also caused divisions within Black communities in the diaspora. But without the acknowledgement of African commercial involvement in the slave trade in the enquiry, a history would present a simplistic binary of malign white Europeans and benign Black Africans.

Although this chapter comes first in our historical enquiries, it was the last of the six we prepared for this book. Our 'felt difficulty' was to bring race to the forefront of a topic without teachers feeling too uncomfortable to use the enquiry. Issues of race are seldom debated in schools these days. Equalities frameworks are in place in schools, and overt racism is taken seriously. But students receive little education about race in classrooms; neither is there sustained professional development for teachers on race equality. Our enquiry into the transatlantic slave trade and New World slavery was an attempt to contribute to students', and possibly teachers', understanding of race.

Historical perspective: the origins and growth of New World slavery

The Arawaks who originally inhabited the islands of Barbados were the first indigenous Americans to come into contact with Europeans. On his first voyage of discovery in 1492, Christopher Columbus described the people he met there in a letter to his patrons, the King and Queen of Spain, as:

> So tractable, [and] so peaceable that I swear to your Majesties
> there is not in the world a better nation. They love their neighbours
> as themselves, and their discourse is ever sweet and gentle, and
> accompanied with a smile; and though it is true that they are
> naked their manners are decorous and praiseworthy.
>
> (Columbus, quoted in Brown, 1991: 1)

Although Columbus was greeted with great kindness by this tribe, other indigenous people he encountered were hostile. Columbus and the Europeans with whom he travelled and corresponded regarded all the 'Indians' (as he termed them), whatever their demeanour, as not fully human. The gentle Arawaks, Columbus observed, would make excellent slaves. The 'Indian' was categorized as either a noble savage who could be put to work, or a wild beast who at best could be tamed and at worst should be exterminated (Fredrickson, 2002).

During a 1519 debate hosted by the Spanish crown in Valladolid, Bartolomeo De Las Casas, a Spanish priest, denounced the seemingly limitless rapacity of the conquistadors and the depravities that their greed inflicted upon the indigenous American people. He maintained that the Spanish had no right to enslave the native people and that the arguments the colonists put forth to justify their subjugation served merely to justify their own avarice. De Las Casas refuted the claim that the 'Indians' were not fully human, recognizing their complex social structure, devotion to their gods and ability to speak several languages as proof of their humanity. He argued that it was therefore the duty of the Spanish to trade peacefully and evangelize them. In an ill-conceived attempt to put an end to the catastrophic depopulation of the Americas, De Las Casas convinced the Spanish royal authorities that to save the Indians the Spanish ought to 'use Africans [for slaves] instead' (Blackburn, 2010). De Las Casas would live to regret his myopic solution.

Spain's neighbour and rival Portugal had recently made the trade in African slaves both practical and profitable. The Portuguese encounters with the peoples of the west coast of Africa were important social contacts between two civilizations; the initial caution and curiosity led to the establishment of permanent trading outposts along the coast, and with that the beginnings of a racist system of trade. Zurara, royal chronicler to Prince Henry the Navigator, in his mid-fifteenth-century writings demonstrated such attitudes during the Portuguese exploration of the west coast of Africa (Blackburn, 2010). Zurara described the Portuguese exploration of Africa in detail and his distinction between 'white Moors' (Arabs) and 'black Moors'

(Muslim Africans) is the first written record identifying the Black Africans whom the Portuguese encountered as the targets of the Biblical curse by Noah that condemned the sons of Ham to slavery. Verse 25 in Chapter 9 of the book of Genesis does not associate Ham's descendants with any group that could be identified in medieval Europe, which is perhaps why it was long used to justify the lowly status of the serf in northern European feudal societies. The convenient Western application of the Hamitic myth to Africans is proof that the Portuguese, and later the Spanish, Dutch and British, did not become slavers because they were racists; they became racists because they had become slavers.

Trevor Burnard wrote that Africans left the shores of West Africa on board slave ships to emerge in the New World as 'negroes', while Europeans stepped off these same vessels as no longer Dutchmen, Scotsmen or Englishmen but as 'white men'. The story of transatlantic slavery thus cannot be detached from the construction and entrenchment of white identity. In *The Invention of the White Race* Theodore W. Allen wrote that the concept of a 'white race' had been invented by the ruling class as a mechanism of social control in response to their fear of growing labour solidarity in the late seventeenth century (Allen, 2012). There had before been mass-scale use of slave labour without an explicit racialized rationale: it is believed that a third of imperial Rome's inhabitants were slaves. These people, however, were mostly the spoils of war. Their bondage came about as a result of their home nations' resistance to Roman authority. The clothes they wore and the tags around their necks, not the colour of their skin, was what identified them as slaves. In the Americas, where in some places slaves accounted for nine-tenths of the population, the social structure was clearer; there were those who had come from Europe of their own will and those who came from Africa in bondage. The so-called 'Peculiar Institution' of racial slavery then became entrenched throughout the eighteenth century and into the nineteenth as the profitability of the crops that slaves cultivated and processed increased. The profits generated from the slave plantations were great, and the wealth was divided amongst the small number of Europeans. Race was born, states Allen, to preserve this arrangement.

In her work on the myths of race in America from the beginning of the colonial era to the present, Jacqueline Jones (2013) asks, 'Who benefitted from the narratives of racial difference and under what conditions?' She cites numerous examples of social and legal interaction between African slaves and white Europeans from the early colonial period of the seventeenth century that suggest that race played little part in the origin of slavery in the future United States. However, Africans were vulnerable to enslavement at a time when labour was desperately needed in the New World. The Africans who cultivated the prized cash crops the New World produced in ever-greater abundance were later said to be naturally suited to slavery. By the late eighteenth century racism was the principal handmaiden to the slave trade and slavery – and it was to outlive it and continue to thrive.

The abolition of the slave trade in 1807 and the ending of slavery in British colonies in 1833 did not put an end to racism; this would have been far too costly for the planters who now had to use emancipated labour to cultivate and export their crops. It was against this backdrop that Victorian thinker and essayist Thomas Carlyle wrote his infamous *Occasional Discourse on the Negro Question* in 1849, published as a pamphlet four years later as *Occasional Discourse on the Nigger Question*. In it Carlyle describes the 'plight' of the white planter of the British West Indies, no longer able to make a decent living due to the naïve philanthropic efforts of the abolitionists (Holt, 1992). The emancipated peoples of the West Indies had been better off under slavery, according to Carlyle, as they lacked the intellect or ethic to make good use of their newly acquired liberty. One passage from his essay makes use of the long-standing racist stereotype of the 'lazy negro':

> Sitting yonder with their beautiful muzzles up to the ears in pumpkins, imbibing sweet pulps and juices; the grinder and incisor teeth ready for every new work, and the pumpkins cheap as grass in those rich climates: while the sugar crops rot ... because labor cannot be hired, so cheap are the pumpkins.
>
> (Carlyle, quoted in Semmel, 1962: 9)

Jamaica was undeniably no longer as profitable for the British as it had been during slavery, but what Carlyle omitted to mention in his essay were the deteriorating economic and political conditions on the island. From emancipation in 1834 to the 1940s the Black population in the British Caribbean remained almost completely disenfranchised despite outnumbering white residents 32 to 1 (Holt, 1992). They had little access to land and were paid poorly for work on white-owned plantations. Between 1855 and 1865 cholera and smallpox plagued the island and several plantations went bankrupt. The Black population of Jamaica began to organize themselves to petition the authorities in London to give them access to disused Crown lands. When one Black Jamaican was arrested for trespassing on a long-abandoned plantation, his community responded by protesting outside the courthouse. This sparked a chain of events that led to a disproportionate response from the British authorities under the

Governor of the Island, Edward Eyre. The soldiers he dispatched to arrest the ringleaders of the courthouse disruption fired indiscriminately, killing men, women and children – 489 in all. The slaughter came to be known as 'The Killing Time' (Holt, 1992). The reactions to the slaughter in London were perhaps as shocking as the killings themselves. Alongside Carlyle, some of Britain's most prominent establishment figures, including Charles Dickens, supported Eyre's actions. To them the Black man was incapable of governing himself and needed to be ruled with an iron rod. Though such coarse racism was challenged by many intellectuals, among them John Stuart Mill, it seems emancipation could not be carried to completion because it exceeded the capacity of white people to think of Black people as equals (Fredrickson, 2002).

The New World slavery enquiry

At the heart of the historical enquiry described below is the construction of race and the power relations that characterized the slave societies of the New World. The focal question was: 'To what extent did New World Slavery turn Africans into Negroes?' This drew on Trevor Burnard's words:

> Africans went on board (the slave ship) as Africans, and emerged in the New World as 'negroes'. Sailors were hired as labourers in Europe, but became 'white men' on the coast of Africa and on board the floating prison of the slave ship.
>
> (Burnard, 2011: 89)

Burnard reminds us that not only did slavery racialize Black people, but white people too were marked out, albeit to their political and economic advantage. The 'familiar' element (Wineburg, 2001) for this enquiry needed to centre on race, so we sought to highlight the way race still determines personal experience and social interactions. We were aware of the contemporary social phenomenon of 'racial profiling': assumptions made about someone's likely behaviour according to their perceived racial identity. Our Black male students were more likely to incur suspicion in public spaces than their white or Asian peers.

We chose a notorious recent example of racial profiling as the 'hook' for the enquiry. In July 2009 Henry Louis Gates, an African-American Harvard professor, was arrested at his home: Gates had locked himself out of his home and someone who saw him 'breaking in' to it had called the police. Initially critical of the attending police officer's overreaction, the then-new US President, Barack Obama, became involved in the affair. He brought Professor Gates and the police officer together over beers at the

White House with himself and Vice-President Joe Biden (Khan *et al.*, 2009) and told them that he wanted the affair to become a 'teachable moment'. We hope our New World slavery enquiry respects the significance of this event and uses it to shape vital lessons for young people. President Obama had probably hoped the meeting would provoke some mutual reflection by the white police officer and the Black academic, and that both parties would be more circumspect in future encounters and slower to react with the anger they had shown. We, however, want students to realize the extent to which people's constructions and assumptions about race penetrate the world on both sides of the Atlantic; to question how these constructs arose; and to consider how particular societies should take more responsibility for them.

History teacher colleagues have told us that they assumed racism prefaced the development of the transatlantic slave trade, before realizing that this notion was not based on historical research. They are surprised when we explain that, as James Walvin put it, Europeans 'didn't become slave traders because of racism, they became racist because of the slave trade' (Walvin, 2000; *Racism: A History*, 2007), but they see that it makes sense. In this enquiry, we interrupt the psyches of both students and teachers by presenting the image of the Black African knight Saint Maurice (see Figure 2.1 and Chapter 3).

Figure 2.1: The statue of Saint Maurice in Magdeburg Cathedral, Germany (authors' image)

The power of this revelation was evident in our own experience of digging into this history. Surrounded by volumes of interpretations of New World slavery, and debating the shape of the enquiry, Robin mentioned the character of Saint Maurice, assuming Abdul had heard of him, but – despite his depth of knowledge of medieval military history – Abdul had not, and was excited to encounter a fellow Black African figure in the midst of medieval Europe. We immediately recognized the power and significance of this figure for the enquiry, presenting our students with this challenge to the pervasive racial profiling of the twenty-first century. It prompted them to ask 'When did these attitudes change?' and 'Was it connected to slavery?'

We introduced the concept of race and its construction in the first lesson of the enquiry. Next, we explored how the Iberian societies began Europe's involvement in buying African slaves in the fifteenth century. Once we had looked at the developing ideas of race and the early justifications for enslavement, we found ourselves confronted with the logic of having to present a lesson on the Middle Passage. This was the feature we considered most dubious in current school history, so we had to find a device to communicate the features of the abomination in a new way. The conventional devices of empathy appeared bereft of usefulness, and Burnard's interpretation (2011: 90) explains why: 'The Middle Passage was a kind of purgatory, in which people were temporarily suspended from being people… [It was a] process of dehumanisation.'

The concept of empathy is vital for scholars of history if they are to understand the human perspectives of people in past societies and situations, but how can you employ empathy to understand people who have become *dehumanized*? We realized through Burnard's ideas why we so disliked the empathy exercises used in history lessons to get students to 'imagine what the slaves were feeling and thinking'. It wasn't so much the implausibility of an illiterate person writing a diary, as such empathy tasks often instruct students to do; it was the impossibility of the attempt to understand human emotions and the feelings of someone who had been torn from the world of humanity in unimaginable torment and squalor.

We decided to focus our attention on trying to understand the impact the Middle Passage could have had on the Africans who survived and became slave labourers in the New World. We considered the concern nowadays about people who experience massive trauma in war situations or violence in civilian life, and researched the condition of Post-Traumatic Stress Disorder (PTSD). We found that psychiatrists have begun to analyse the plight of people in historical situations in the light of what is now known about PTSD. R.J. Daly investigated the case of Samuel Pepys and his reactions to the Great Fire of London, and concluded that Pepys's diary gives clear evidence of PTSD (Daly, 1983). It seemed clear to us that Africans emerging into the New World as Negroes in perpetual slavery were certain to suffer terrible after-effects of the Atlantic crossing; asking students to examine evidence from contemporary sources about the experiences of the African slaves in the Middle Passage in light of what we told them about PTSD could help them to understand the impact of the journey more clinically, but without losing the sense of horror and abomination. This was the heart of the enquiry, and at the end of the double lesson came an exercise in which we asked the students to critique an activity undertaken in Durham in 2007 with primary school children, who were asked to lie down on a full-size plan of an eighteenth-century slave ship drawn on the grass in the university grounds. The students questioned the educational value of such 'fun' learning activities by applying their sophisticated understanding of the issue gained from the discussions on empathy and PTSD.

The other daunting challenge in the planning of this enquiry was African complicity in the operation of the slave trade. We had researched certain aspects of African slavery, and recognized the differences between its historical features in West Africa, with its ties to warfare and the treatment of war captives, and slavery in the New World of the Americas. Examining the history of Ghana's Gold Coast, we came across Philip Quaque (or Kweku). Our first research revealed a worthy character, an eighteenth-century Black African man raised by English people in London and educated in Islington. Quaque was ordained an Anglican priest at St James's Palace in Westminster; he travelled to West Africa as a missionary to both African and British-origin residents (Carretta and Reese, 2010). Quaque appeared to be another example of the type of 'worthy African' who lived and prospered in England long before the migrations of the later twentieth century, comparable to Ignatius Sancho and Olaudah Equiano (Fryer, 1985). This narrative was rudely disturbed, however, by the discovery that Quaque was intimately connected with the operation of the slave trade on the Gold Coast: his community 'father' (sponsor) was Birempon Cudjoe, a prominent African leader in the operation of slave commerce, and Quaque's opportunities in London had come about through a treaty between Cudjoe and the British (Holsey, 2008). Quaque's story now became rather complex and he no longer appeared to be unequivocally heroic. We decided to present this dilemma to the students in our enquiry and let them debate the moral tensions that characterize such stories.

Students frequently want to know why the Africans didn't resist the imposition of slavery. The brutal weaponry of the slave traders offers some explanation, but it is also the case that many captives did resist. Throwing themselves overboard during the crossing was one form of resistance. There were also rebellions on the coasts of Africa and even on board the slave ships, although these were short-lived. It was on the Caribbean islands that enslaved Africans stood a better chance of successful revolt, although not on the small islands where the authorities could easily track down runaways. It was on the largest of the British West Indian islands, Jamaica, and on the mainland territory of Guiana, that communities of runaway Africans managed to establish themselves as free societies. These escapees were termed 'Maroons', from the Spanish *cimmarón*, meaning 'fugitive' or 'runaway'.

We decided to end the enquiry with attention to this alternative fate for some Africans, in becoming Maroons rather than Negroes. But their status as heroes is open to debate. The British attempted to fight the Maroons, and in Jamaica there was a long period of conflict from the late seventeenth century until 1739 when the British decided that they should sign a treaty with these rebellious Africans whom they could not conquer. This treaty entailed compromise: although the Maroons secured their autonomy on the island, they had to agree to collaborate with the British authorities by returning any runaway slaves from the plantations. Historian Philip Morgan discusses the constant interplay between accommodation and resistance, so often characteristic of Black people's lives in the British Empire (Morgan, 2004). It is important for students to understand that the forging of race and power made white Europeans formidable masters in the New World.

Table 2.1 Outline of the seven-lesson enquiry on New World slavery

How far did New World slavery turn Africans into Negroes?

Lesson 1: Where do ideas of 'race' come from?	*Summary:* The lesson presents the students with notions of race, moving from the familiar experiences of racial profiling in contemporary societies to the presence of a Black heroic medieval knight in Europe, which interrupts the psyche and prompts the students to ask questions about the history of race and slavery. The lesson ends with an exploration of names, focusing on the term 'Negro' and its origins in European encounters with Africans through the slave trade.

Activities include: Using a video clip of news reports from July 2009, we look at Harvard Professor Henry Louis Gates, who was subject to racial profiling when arrested for causing a disturbance by breaking into his own home; it includes an interview with former US Secretary of State General Colin Powell, who also suffered racial profiling as an African American. A video clip and image of the statue of Saint Maurice in Magdeburg Cathedral prompts a discussion about early European thinking about Black Africans. Students consider questions they would want to ask about the history of race as an idea, and are introduced to the enquiry question itself.

Lesson 2: When did Europeans become involved in trading African slaves?	*Summary:* This lesson explores the emergence of the Iberian powers in the fifteenth century, and their role in establishing the

European slave trade on the West African coast. The ideas of the Portuguese chronicler Zurara and the Spanish priest Bartolomeo De Las Casas are used to suggest that Europeans struggled with the emergence of notions of race, Africans and human exploitation. Links between the Christian faith and the development of racism are found in the Hamitic Myth and in the judgements of the Papacy, which seem to seal the fate of Black African peoples during this period.

Activities include: Studying a map of the Atlantic world in the 1450s and the developing trade connections across Europe, Africa and the Americas involving Portugal and Spain. Examining written sources from Zurara about the 'Moors' of Africa, and the distinction he perceived between 'white Moors' and 'black Moors'. An extract from De Las Casas reveals his judgement about using Black African slaves instead of the native Americans.

Lessons 3 and 4: What is exceptional about the Middle Passage?

Summary: The central part of the enquiry focuses on the core aspect of the process by which African people became a different kind of living being, termed 'Negroes', after they were enslaved and transported in the 'Middle Passage'. Shunning overtly empathetic approaches, the phenomenon is studied more clinically, emphasizing the impact the Middle Passage would have had on the Africans transported. What did enslaved Africans experience after the Atlantic sea journey, following their incarceration on the African coast? The students are asked to critique current pedagogical practices where young people are given practical activities to empathize directly with enslaved Africans.

Activities include: Studying five sources, largely produced by anti-slavery campaigners, about the Middle Passage, using them to make an assessment of enslaved Africans and Post-Traumatic Stress Disorder. There is one short video clip about the trade, plus pictures and texts. Students are introduced to Burnard's interpretation of the development of race that lies behind the wording of the overall enquiry question; they are beginning to frame answers to the enquiry. This section ends with evaluating a picture of Durham primary school children in 2007 lying on a full-size plan of a slave ship.

Lesson 5: How did Philip Quaque become a Reverend and not a Negro?

Summary: The most challenging of the lessons explores issues concerning the involvement of African people in the slave trade. The message is that the situation is complex and messy, and the purpose is not to pass judgement on anyone involved. Slowly revealing the story of

Philip Quaque exposes this complexity, and the likely sympathies with Quaque change as more about his background is revealed: from being rather heroic as a pioneer African in London, he then becomes the direct beneficiary of African slaving on the Gold Coast. What is clear is that the Africans were not directly responsible for the horrors of the Middle Passage. There is also a difference between the operation of slavery in the African polities and the European commerce, the former being closely tied to warfare and the fate of prisoners. Some students may find this issue uncomfortable; teachers need to be sensitive.

Activities include: Consider the story of Philip Quaque in three stages, and examine the idea of significance each time. The final account shows his connection to the slave trade and Caboceer Cudjoe, and students should debate what difference that makes to their thinking about him. There are two paintings that suggest different interpretations of the workings of the trade on the African coast and also a section that examines the connection between African warfare and slave trading.

Lesson 6: How were New World plantations slave societies, not merely societies *with slaves*?

Summary: New World slavery is the focus: we examine the hierarchy of Caribbean societies in the era of slavery and how it was constructed entirely on race and colour. The key point is to emphasize that New World plantation societies were different to other world societies that had used slavery before this time; the latter were societies *with* slaves, but in the New World one found entire slave societies. The basis of English authority and imposition of servitude, too, was race.

Activities include: An exploration of a painting by gradually revealing the full scene, which shows a plantation on the island of Antigua in the shadow of the European fort on the hill behind. The first image is of a well-dressed Black man, akin to the caboceer of the last lesson, and gradually it becomes clear that this man has no real authority and appears to be being used by the white plantation owner to control the other slave labourers. A tiered hierarchy diagram is the final resource for the lesson; it shows the division of people into negroes, mulattoes and blancs.

Lesson 7: How did Negroes become Maroons in Jamaica and were they really free?

Summary: The final lesson offers a contrast to the grim narrative of racial slavery from the bulk of the enquiry, and describes some successful resistance. In the Caribbean islands slaves seized opportunities to run away and in remote areas they stood a chance of avoiding recapture; they formed *Maroon* societies. Complexity emerges again, though, because the Maroons of Jamaica signed treaties with the British that guaranteed Maroon autonomy in exchange for their agreement to return runaway slaves from then on. The British betrayed the Maroons in the outcome of the Second Maroon War in 1798, and some exiled Maroons ended up in Sierra Leone in Africa. Even resistance proves to be 'messy', and the students have plenty of opportunity to debate and develop more subtle understandings of situations throughout.

Activities include: Exploring the story of Nanny of the Maroons, and how she became Jamaica's only female national hero. Considering the balance of warfare and diplomacy in the success of the Maroons in the eighteenth century. Learning the final story of the outcome of the Second Maroon War in 1798 and the way in which the British authorities tricked the Maroons into final surrender, then exiled many of them to Nova Scotia and then back to Africa in Sierra Leone. Had the Maroons escaped the fate of other enslaved brethren and kept their dignity and respect as Africans?

Transforming the learning and teaching of New World slavery

Race was clearly established as the core substantive concept of our enquiry into the history of the enslavement of African peoples by Europeans and the transatlantic trade, which grew astronomically from the sixteenth to the nineteenth centuries. This meant that teachers and students could not skirt around the issue, so developing the enquiry was challenging. Furthermore, we felt there were major problems in the way slavery was taught in schools, particularly for students of direct or diasporic African heritage (Traille, 2007). We would have preferred to steer clear of these multiple challenges, but once we grasped the task in the spring of 2015, we were glad we did, as the potential for a transformation of Black history in school really does hinge on teachers being able to address their teaching of slavery. As yet the enquiry has been taught only once, and we have no data from students, but their teacher gave us a thorough evaluation of the lessons.

The enquiry was taught to Year 9 students (14-year-olds) at a small Catholic boys' school just south of London; over 50 per cent of students came from African-Caribbean backgrounds. Juan, their Hispanic-heritage teacher, recognized the sensitivity of the enquiry and realized he would have to devote significant lesson time to exploring identity and give his students the chance to become comfortable exploring their own connections to race before exploring race and its association with slavery. The evidence suggests that the risks involved in tackling such a controversial subject were justified and the students' engagement with the enquiry was strong from the start. Juan wrote:

> The boys were slightly uncomfortable at first (particularly with the first two clips), but seemed to understand why we were showing them. The familiar to strange [progression] provided a great space to discuss and explore the concept of racial profiling, challenge stereotypes and explore the extent to which people might be 'racist'. Some of the African boys raised the way in which they have been mistreated in the past in shops or areas. The boys were very comfortable sharing their stories and people respected what was being shared.
>
> (Juan, history teacher)

The initial discomfort seemed to suggest that the students were taking the subject seriously, which was positive, and their growing confidence in the context of the enquiry was apparent in future lessons.

A key part of the enquiry process is to open up opportunities for students to question and think through issues for themselves. In the area of race this can make teachers feel vulnerable, especially white teachers in a multiracial school. Though such teachers might want to be able to meet the needs of all their students, Black students will sometimes benefit from talking over issues with Black adults. Juan recognized this and explains part of the process that ensued at his school:

> I was delighted to hear that a few students had gone to see the French teacher, who is from the Democratic Republic of the Congo (DRC), to discuss a few topics from the lesson. I have realized that the teaching of such contentious and sensitive issues requires the teacher to be accessible. Some of the African students have found the study of the enquiry very interesting, but one also notices that they want to delve deeper into certain topics and controversies in a safe setting.
>
> (Juan, history teacher)

Such open dialogue might not always be possible within a school, but the teacher can encourage students to engage with their family and community in discussions and bring those ideas back into the classroom. New World slavery offers no easy answers, so creating opportunities for open, non-judgemental discussion is vital.

This is the only enquiry in the book we have not yet taught, and we look forward to doing so. It is the one that makes the explicit connection with the construction of race in the British context and invites the students to make use of their sense of the construction of race in their own lives. Juan suggests that this is an aspect of history that needs further exploration:

> One final thought is that it struck me during the course of the enquiry that the boys wanted to talk about current issues of race. I think it is a very powerful enquiry, but somehow we might have to bring it back to the beginning: how has the past affected racial relationships? The boys felt comfortable talking about discrimination and racism. However, it might be good to even make a clearer connection. It could perhaps be a new enquiry altogether.
>
> (Juan, history teacher)

The dynamic interaction between the study of the past and the challenges of contemporary society is critical to the position of history in the school curriculum (Barton, 2009). We hope that fellow history educators will take up Juan's suggestion and develop further enquiries for their students that explore the issues of race through the centuries. Other chapters in this book offer suggestions as to how that can be done.

Chapter 3

The story of Timbuktu

The challenge of contemporary myths about Africa

According to Henry Louis Gates Jr, the notion of 'Africa' conjures thoughts of 'poverty and flies' (*In Our Time*, 1999) in many Westerners' minds today. Such thoughts take no account of the great advances made in many African nations and confirm the persistent European and American phenomenon of denying the significance and even existence of Africa's history. Disturbingly, such negative views of Africa and its history are not confined to right-wing white communities and social groups; Black people too absorb negative notions of African poverty and underdevelopment. Robin's godson has proud, professional British Black African parents and attended a multicultural primary school that was careful to promote positive views of the diverse heritages of its children, yet by the age of seven he believed that people in Africa lived in mud huts and did not enjoy the comforts of Western living. His mother had to take him on a trip to Nigeria to dispel these beliefs; only solid evidence would convince him to the contrary.

A year later we were at a session in the British Museum at which a leading museum educator from their Africa Gallery declared that, since he dealt mainly with primary school children, he did not face the challenges of racist thinking he expected in older students. We were shocked at this assumption – Robin's godson's experience illustrates how issues of race, history and Africa need to be tackled from an early age. Some of the myths about Africa aren't learned at home or school, but appear to spring from encounters in playgrounds or parks. The naiveté of the British Museum curator may seem harmlessly optimistic, but if he fails to recognize the challenges that are already emerging in the mind-sets of his young visitors, he has to share the responsibility for the perpetual grip these ideas have on society. Alternative narratives of African history are urgently needed to establish authentic, positive views of the continent's past.

Black history is intrinsically African, and its curriculum in schools should be concerned with the historical interpretations of that continent. Black history cannot deal only with the African American or Caribbean past and the transatlantic slave trade; doing justice to Black history must do justice to African history. However, teaching the history of the African continent is very challenging, particularly in the Western, Atlantic nations that were involved in the enslavement and colonization of Africans. Alongside those exploitative processes, almost all traces of the history of Africa before European encroachment were expunged. Despite the available written sources by medieval Muslim chroniclers such as Al Bekri and Ibn Battuta, interpretations of Africa as a 'Dark Continent' spread through the Western world from the eighteenth century onwards (Davidson, 1992). Legacies of these unjust distortions of history still permeate our societies, creating alienation and division.

There are sometimes disputes in school about who is entitled to call themselves 'Black'. Abdul overheard a small group of A-Level students talking about issues of identity; a Caribbean student told off a girl of Somali heritage for identifying herself as 'Black', demanding a much narrower phenotypical criterion that would exclude her. As recent arrivals in the UK, Somali people are often resented and rejected, not only because of their recent arrival but also because some modern historians of sub-Saharan Africa have downplayed the significant contribution made to the world by the Horn of Africa. Somalia's story is sometimes considered part of the history of the Middle East and the Indian Ocean, rather than continental Africa. Somalis' identities as Muslim and African can exacerbate their exclusion: they face Islamophobia as well as racism. A school history curriculum requires historical enquiries across the history of Africa before the arrival of Europeans that feature the great civilizations and the centuries of peaceful and respectful integration of Islam into Africa.

The idea of a common heritage of African history that predates the encounters with European slave traders could help to affirm the identity of students whose heritage is connected to the African continent and thus inspire greater unity. In our enquiry into the history of Timbuktu, South African conservator Alexio Motsi speaks about discovering the history of the city's ancient manuscripts and declares that the knowledge made him 'more proud to be an African'. Indeed, in light of renewed evidence that human beings have their origin on the continent of Africa thousands of years ago (Meredith, 2011), the exploration of millennia of African civilizations can be a source of pride for all students. Our historical enquiries introduce stories of positive achievement by people of African descent, such as the Asante Empire in West Africa, and the contribution of Somali people to the British Empire. The struggles of Black peoples against Western exploitation and oppression will feature prominently in a balanced account of the centuries of Black history but should not be the only narrative. Unfortunately, our research discussions with students suggest that they have already formed a narrower view of Black history.

According to many of our students it is the element of struggle and interaction with Europeans that marks out certain history as distinctly 'Black'. This was especially prominent in discussions about an enquiry focused on European encounters with the Asante Kingdom in West Africa, during which students referred to the central role of the excesses of colonialism in Africa. Carl, an African-Caribbean student in a Central London boys' comprehensive, said, 'For something to be a part of Black history it has to involve white people trying to take things from them [Black people].' Struggles against racism were seen as the vital element in Black History Month. In distinguishing between aspects of our British Somali enquiry (see Chapter 7), Khalid, a Somali student in a North London school, picked out elements that involved racial conflicts as Black history and explained that 'for Black History Month it's only about racism that happened, like Martin Luther King, Nelson Mandela, he was imprisoned, that's all racism and stuff, like, most of it is racism'.

Accounts of valiant Black struggles are important, and the leadership of King and Mandela can inspire belief in a world where racism would not be allowed to impede Black citizens. However, these struggles still suggest the primacy of white Western civilizations in world history, and they don't point to the existence of longstanding independent African civilizations. Obscuring and denying that reality is one strategy of Western oppression. Doing justice to Black history should involve history teachers in actively uncovering Africa's lost narratives, as well as teaching about the triumphs of Black struggles.

Historical perspective: the development of African historiography

E. H. Carr wrote in 1961 that the historian would always find the facts they want; this goes some way toward explaining why African history was missing from European historical scholarship for hundreds of years. From the late seventeenth century up to the height of decolonization in the 1960s Europe was interested in Africa only inasmuch as it could exploit it. Acknowledgement of Africa's history might have encouraged Europeans to rein in the worst excesses associated with slavery and colonialism. Basil Davidson, author of landmark works on Africa's history and political future, explored the importance of interactions between Africa and Europe in his eight-part documentary 'Africa: The Story of a Continent' (Davidson, 1994). He noted that differences in race were not a source of hostility and distrust during the classic or the medieval eras. Davidson supported his observation with numerous examples, such as the writings of Herodotus. He also noted a statue in Magdeburg Cathedral in Germany of St Maurice, the Black African patron saint of the Holy Roman Empire (see also Chapter 2). Herodotus noted the contributions of Africa to the Greeks, but this knowledge was obscured in modern times. Senegalese historian and anthropologist Cheikh Anta Diop points to the general view amongst historians that Greek civilization owed a great deal to the Egyptians, and criticizes later historians' refusal to accept that the great Nile Valley civilization was 'African' (Diop, 1964).

Serious historians, especially those writing in the twentieth century, had access to evidence that the continent was home to a wealth of sophisticated and sometimes spectacular cultures and civilizations, yet held on doggedly to their preconceptions. When Europeans first saw the magnificent ruins of Great Zimbabwe in the late nineteenth century, they were so blinded by their prejudice that they refused to believe that this immense royal city had anything to do with the Black Africans who lived beside it. They created fantastical stories to explain its origin, with the purpose of denying that these monuments and markers of civilization were built by the Black Africans. By then Africans were almost universally portrayed by Europeans as simple and barbarous. Georg Wilhelm Friedrich Hegel epitomized this attitude in the early nineteenth century when he spoke of the Africans as without a history, in a land shrouded in the darkness of barbarism (Willinsky, 1998).

The pervasiveness of such attitudes informs the work of respected historian Hugh Trevor-Roper, who, as late as the 1960s, wrote that 'there was no real African history'. Kwame Anthony Appiah (1998) reminds us that although Trevor-Roper was an 'uncommon historian' he was thinking with the crowd when he dismissed African history, proceeding from the narrow-minded assumption that history's principal purpose is to document Europe's cultural and political pre-eminence. Such racist and haughty attitudes have dominated the European historiography of the African continent since the Enlightenment. The parallels between the views of Trevor-Roper and Hegel are not coincidental. Both wrote in an intellectual climate where European civilization felt an overwhelming sense of its own achievements. The West, Niall Ferguson explains (2003), had enjoyed a spectacular rise, founded on technological and financial advances that other nations hadn't developed the ability to comprehend, let alone compete with.

This prejudiced construction of Africans often had its own necessity, exemplified in the vast programme of radiocarbon dating in the hills of Mapungubwe in South Africa between 1935 and 1970, after treasures including a famous 'golden rhino' were discovered there. The fascination with this site was not, as one might hope, about understanding a significant earlier African civilization; it was because the Apartheid government of South Africa refused to accept the radiocarbon dating that revealed Black Africans had been present there in the twelfth century, five centuries before Europeans arrived. The belief that white settlers enriched an empty land in the south of the continent was one of the major political justifications for white minority rule in Southern Africa.

Europeans were not always so dismissive of Africans. Located deep in the recesses of European historiography are numerous sources, some dating from the sixteenth and seventeenth centuries, that disturb people's assumptions about the longevity of notions of white supremacy, and challenge the paternalistic attitudes of many Europeans towards Africans. Steven R. Smith (1977) drew on the writings of two Europeans during the Age of Discovery: Englishman Robert Jobson and Dutchman Olfert Dapper. Both travelled across Africa in the hope of acquiring valuable trading links. Smith notes their reluctance to dwell on the differences in the Africans' physical attributes, and how these two men instead describe Africans in much the same way as many of their contemporaries and forerunners described the peoples of the Near and Far East. One must understand that both men had a particular interest in presenting Africans as they saw them. They were explorers who wrote of their experiences in order to attract European investment. Jobson in particular wrote at length about the different religions and customs of the tribes he encountered along the Gold Coast. These two authors' accounts of Africans were complimentary and derogatory in fairly equal measure; neither Jobson nor Dapper, however, presumed that the Africans they encountered were intrinsically inferior to Europeans.

Smith also refers to the writings of Sir Thomas Browne in 1646 on the issue of race; Browne's title 'On Vulgar Errors' is an indication that he intended to take a more rational approach to racial difference. Browne dismissed the notion of skin colour as an indicator of likely behaviour or a determinant of position in society. As a Bible scholar, he chose to focus on the oft-misrepresented story of Ham, used for centuries to justify the enslavement and perpetual servitude of Africans. In the Bible story, Noah's son Ham exposes Noah's nakedness while his father is lying in bed in a drunken state; as a result his progeny are cursed forever to remain in servitude. Browne emphasized the fact that Ham's ethnicity and complexion are not mentioned anywhere in the Old Testament. The inclusion of this story in Browne's 'Vulgar Errors' suggests that some people in his time did regard Black Africans as the descendants of Ham, but he goes on to dismiss the validity of this view by explaining that black skin could not be part of God's curse as Africans saw nothing wrong with the colour of their skin. Browne went on to point out the folly of applying European standards of beauty to Africans.

The issue of race is one of many Browne addressed in what was essentially an encyclopaedia of common misconceptions. He never visited Africa but must have been exposed to some xenophobic views in order to have included them in his book. Fifty years before the publication of this, Browne's most famous work, Queen Elizabeth I had issued a proclamation calling for the expulsion of all Black people in her realm. It seems this decision was driven primarily by economic factors, but also by the high visibility of the few Black people living in England at a time of political and economic uncertainty (Onyeka, 2013). The very presence of free people of African descent in England in the reign of Elizabeth is itself an indication that attitudes towards Africa were not uniform. It is likely that Black people would have been met just as readily with ambivalence as with racial prejudice; some may well have been entertained by people wanting to hear about the fabled and mysterious lands of Africa.

That there were flourishing empires in Africa at the time of Browne's writing is not in dispute; the sophistication of the administrations of the Mali and Songhay Empires had long been recognized by Arab chroniclers writing centuries apart, most notably Al Bekri and Ibn Battuta. The magnificence of the Mali Empire was such that it featured prominently on a series of fourteenth-century maps produced for the Crown of Aragon by Abraham Cresques. One depicts a noble African king in the centre of the continent, elegantly holding an orb and sceptre. How tragic then that such intellectual giants as Trevor-Roper and Hegel ignored Thomas Browne and denied the very notion of Africa as a land worthy of attention, or indeed history. What may have contributed to Trevor-Roper and Hegel's dismissive views was their primitive understanding of what constitutes history and prehistory. The prejudice in their words reflects a disdain not only for Africa and its people but also for any historiography outside white Western culture.

The Timbuktu and African history enquiry

Of the stages of doing justice to Black history that we discussed earlier, our students have generally become involved at the choreography stage, learning through a historical enquiry about the circumstances of a situation in the past. They are usually oblivious to the historiographical struggles that have gone on behind the scenes to do justice to the history, and to the work of the pugilists, who may well have included their own teachers. However, we have in a number of our enquiries focused on changes in historical interpretations, and in this dimension the students have to be introduced to the pugilists' positions in order to appreciate why and how traditional narratives have been challenged. The concept of historical interpretations involves our students directly in doing justice to history, which can be exciting and authentic. Interpretations can show the connections between school history and street mythologies, and thus with debunking those pejorative myths. Students should know that folk knowledge about the primitiveness of Africa has an academic strand associated with it, advanced by some of Europe's most prominent academic figures through the ages. This can be challenging for students, particularly because they have to consider not only the past situation they are studying, such as medieval Zimbabwe, but also the time period of the interpretation they are analysing, such as the 1950s if they are listening to Sir Mortimer Wheeler. The demands of this work have been described as 'double vision' (Card, 2004). This can seem somewhat remote and lacklustre to young history students, so we had to find a way to establish a 'felt difficulty' in this area of historical interpretations.

Our answer was to try to make the issue more personal. We set up an antagonist within the enquiry with whom the students could grapple in successive lessons, considering a range of different situations and sources that could answer the historical questions the antagonist's views might prompt. The students we have been working with in multicultural urban contexts have a strong sense of outrage at situations they deem to be unjust, and particularly those that appear to be racist. So, although our enquiry aims to establish positive narratives about Africa and its histories, particularly before the arrival of Europeans, we decided to start by presenting the students with negative views of Africa and its past, which they could then assail as the enquiry unfolded. This was done with a stunningly crude drawing of four African warriors in an 1884 advertisement for Pears soap. The warriors appear to be worshipping a rock in the wilderness that had the slogan 'Pears Soap is the Best' painted on it. Although they appeared strong and warlike, everything else about them was negative, particularly their apparent ignorance and superstition in bowing down to a rock. The typical late-nineteenth-century view of Africa as a 'Dark Continent' could then be explained, with its connection to justifying colonial occupation and rule.

Next, we used Georg Wilhelm Friedrich Hegel, and his infamous comment about the absence of any history in Africa, as a suitable foil for the students' own studies of African history and civilizations, particularly the story of Great Zimbabwe and its interpretations through the twentieth century. We used a video clip in which Basil Davidson spoke Hegel's words, which we also posted on screen: 'Africa is not a historical part of the world; it is a continent cloaked in darkness'. The impact of Hegel's notions and the 'Dark Continent' idea were considered against interpretations of the ruined city of Great Zimbabwe. We began with the views of white Europeans in the British colony of Rhodesia, where the ruins were found, and ended with recent Black African ideas, explored in a television clip from a documentary by Henry Louis Gates Jr, the Harvard historian who featured in the racial profiling case that opened our slavery enquiry.

To pursue a study in depth of one aspect of hidden African histories, the focus of this enquiry then moved to one town in West Africa whose profile in the Western world over the last two centuries masked its longevity as a renowned centre of learning in the Islamic African world: Timbuktu. This city in Mali has been synonymous for centuries with danger and mystery, and we found a recent television programme from the US, hosted by the intrepid white American, Hunter Ellis, which conveyed this succinctly in its short opening sequence. The idea of the enquiry was to juxtapose this reputation for remote peril with the knowledge that Timbuktu is one of the oldest university towns in the world and that thousands of antique manuscripts survive in its libraries and homes. We used Thabo Mbeki as the foil for Hunter Ellis, because the South African president visited the city in 2001, and committed his country's support for the work of preserving Timbuktu's treasured documents.

The overall enquiry question brought together these two opinions of the city's significance: 'How could there be so much learning at "the end of the earth"?' The manuscripts of Timbuktu were evidence that there was at least one part of the African continent that had not been 'dark' for centuries, and so the exploration of the city became part of the refutation of Hegel as well as solving the mystery of its distorted interpretation in modern times. A special feature of the pedagogy of this enquiry was that we asked the students to each develop their own four questions in light of the conundrum of Timbuktu's reputation. The idea was that their questions would give students a regular focus for reflecting on their learning and engage them as individuals in lessons that were strongly focused on group work activities.

A good deal of the material for this enquiry was found in a BBC television documentary entitled *The Lost Libraries of Timbuktu* (2009), presented by a Black British woman, Aminatta Forna, a writer who spent much of her childhood in Sierra Leone, where her father had been born. Not only did the programme give us important information about the manuscripts and Timbuktu's past; key characters in it infused the history with closer personal connections for the students. A strong sense of the passionate commitment of the French-speaking Black Africans who were caring for the manuscripts and guarding the oral traditions of the city was animatedly conveyed over the subtitles. A scene of the graduation ceremony at Sankore University in Timbuktu was especially memorable: the graduand answers oral questions so he can wear the special turban, the shape of which resembles the Arabic name of God; the speaker demonstrated the initial dramatic whisking of the graduand's old turban from his head. We introduced a simulation of this scene into the enquiry, much to the delight of the students.

Of greater importance was the identity of the programme's experts: all were Black Africans, and they vividly demonstrated the scholarly acumen of their people both now and in the historic manuscripts. This authority and agency countered the portrayal in most school history resources of only white people carrying out historical study, even concerning African subjects. Perhaps the most significant figure was Alexio Motsi, a South African conservator, whom we introduced in the first lesson. He was part of the task force sent following President Mbeki's visit, and the short interview segment we used conveys Motsi's own initial misconceptions about the remote Timbuktu, and contrasts them with his elation over the manuscripts themselves. Motsi said he thought of the manuscripts as 'more than gold', and this was a fine epigram for the students to explain, making a connection in their minds between the gold the city was famed for trading and the scholarly dimension of its historical reputation.

In a podcast discussion with Professor Gates and author Anthony Sampson, Melvin Bragg (*In Our Time*, 1999) challenged the value of the Timbuktu manuscripts if people didn't understand what was written in the medieval Arabic. Gates's initial response was to point out that part of the documents' significance lay not only in their content but in their very existence as written texts, as this challenged Western preconceptions about Africa. The whole 'Dark Continent' narrative depended in part on the idea that Africa had no literate culture and so its history could be dismissed. Moreover, since Bragg made his provocative challenge, a great deal of work has been done in accessing and translating the material in the manuscripts of Timbuktu, and the enquiry devotes a lesson to exploring facets of what was recorded there.

The essential connection between Islam and the growth of wisdom and knowledge at Timbuktu is paramount in the manuscripts, and this presents another possible 'interruption of the psyche' for twenty-first century students. They are showered with stereotypes of aggressive Muslims, rooted in notions of 'jihad', of a religion spread by the sword (Whitaker, 2004), but they learn that the flourishing of Islam in Timbuktu and the Empire of Mali owed nothing to Muslim warriors, but came with the growth of trade. The enquiry explores some of the content of the manuscripts and their connection to Muslim practices, including astronomical texts that connect with the observance of prayer times and direction, and others that address more commonplace concerns: a recipe for toothpaste shows how oral hygiene was important for communal religious practice. Furthermore, there is discussion of the idea that Islam connected with African traditions in Timbuktu, producing an integration of cultures that one of the revered local scholars calls 'a tolerant Islam'.

The enquiry also explores aspects of the political life of this significant medieval African city, although this proved challenging. The digging process for this enquiry was more challenging than any of the others described in this book, since neither of us had studied the city's history before, and the literature available was very specialized (Saad, 2010). It is always a dilemma for history teachers to know how much to simplify the material they are presenting to students, and what to leave out (Kitson *et al.*, 2011). Often teachers rely on textbooks to help them decide, going usually to the book suitable for the level above the one they are about to teach. But for the history of Timbuktu the resources were either highly erudite academic tomes or simple, colourful texts for primary-school children. We decided to concentrate on exploring the mode of government that appeared to be found in Timbuktu, which connected to the idea of its intellectual foundations; as it was Timbuktu's scholars who undertook political decision-making, we termed the city government an 'epistocracy'. Saad's (2010) analyses clearly indicated Timbuktu as a city of scholars, so we used this term to define the regime as 'rule by the knowers'. Epistocracy appears to be a relatively young word, and we may not be applying it in the way it was intended by Estlund (2003), but it was a term we could use as a contrast to other, better-known political concepts, including democracy and autocracy, to help students see differences in the way states are governed.

Our students generally relish learning complex new vocabulary, as long as it is introduced with clarity and relevance. Popular culture is strongly influenced by the use of lyrics in hip-hop and other musical forms where verbal jousting is acclaimed (Lamont Hill, 2009), and a term learned in a history lesson could appear in a lyrical contest that evening. Young people might also recognize that complex vocabulary, like 'epistocracy', marks a person out as intellectual and they appreciate being trusted with its use. Such vocabulary was frequently developed in a course Robin taught on multicultural British history after 1945 (Whitburn and Yemoh, 2012), as we discuss further in Chapter 6; one of his students, David, commented about the work:

> Knowing your history could separate you from being an intellectual and a common person … You are more of an intellectual if you know history, especially in this class. Everyone in the class is linked together somehow. People you thought you would never be friends with. It's just professional; you share your opinions.
>
> (Bishop's High School student David)

David's initial comment might seem divisive within his mixed ability class, but the separation he implied was not between himself and fellow students who were working at lower levels of attainment but from people who choose to remain ignorant of history, and whom he calls 'common'. Teachers might be loath to expect some students to learn words that don't fit into their general lexicon. They probably wouldn't think twice about introducing complex terms to children with rich cultural capital, but we argue that students from less advantaged backgrounds can also be given terms like this, although they might need more guidance and support in using them appropriately.

The final lesson of the enquiry looks at the decline of Timbuktu, particularly following the invasion by Morocco in the late sixteenth century. One of the city's scholars, Ahmed Baba, chose to surrender to the Moroccans and was sent into captivity in Morocco, but steadfastly refused to assimilate into Moroccan society and wouldn't work as a scholar for the enemies of his home city. The importance of Baba's identity as a Black African scholar is brought out in a filmed interview with a contemporary scholar of Timbuktu, Salem Ould Al Hajj. He claims that Ahmed Baba insisted on being known in Morocco as 'As-Sudani' – that is, 'Black man'. Ahmed Baba did eventually return to Timbuktu, and one of the city's most important contemporary centres of learning today is called the Ahmed Baba Institute. Baba was famous for promoting a learned phrase sometimes ascribed to the prophet Muhammad: 'The ink of the scholar is more precious than the blood of the martyr.' We felt that this phrase brought out some of the important ideas developed at this scholarly centre, and accounted for the anomaly of how 'so much learning' could be present in a city that was given such a distorted reputation by the West, so we asked the students to finish their enquiry by designing a poster around this phrase.

Table 3.1 Outline of the eight-lesson enquiry on the historiography of Africa and Timbuktu

How 'dark' was the story of Africa before 1900? How was there so much learning at 'the end of the earth'?

| Lesson 1: What did British people think of Africa before 1900? | *Summary:* An introductory lesson to the overall theme of African historiography and the negative assumptions made about Africa and its people by Western |

societies during the modern era. There will be general myths and stereotypes about African history, even where many students come from an African background. The interpretation given by Hegel provides the epitome of the modern derogation of African history that could underpin not only the African slave trade, but also the systematic colonization and exploitation of the lands of Africa from the late nineteenth into the twentieth century.

Activities include: Students begin with a short activity that confirms the contemporary commonplace ideas about African society (what Gates calls 'poverty and flies') through an 'odd-one-out' exercise, where the picture of impoverished Black people is actually the non-African picture, being a shot from the Deep South of the US. The ambiguity in the Pears soap advert gets the students thinking more deeply than would a very blatantly racist nineteenth-century image of Black people. They finally listen to Hegel's dismissal of Africa, and consider what he based his claim on, considering he had never been to Africa.

| Lesson 2: How did interpretations of Great Zimbabwe change during the twentieth century? | *Summary:* The example of the ruins of the ancient city of Great Zimbabwe is presented in three different |

interpretations from the 1930s, 1950s and 1980s. The idea that this obviously spectacular monument to a great civilization could not have been built by Black Africans is shown clearly in a travel poster, dated 1938. Then a Mortimer Wheeler film clip from 1958 shows some changes in the interpretation, although the approach is again strongly paternalistic and sceptical of the prowess of any Black African society at the site. Finally, a 1998 interpretation given by Henry Louis Gates shows that in recent times there has been a much more positive approach to the idea of Black African civilization, coinciding with the major political change constituted by Zimbabwe's independence in 1980.

Activities include: Considering the ghostly figure of the Queen of Sheba given in a colonial Rhodesian view of the ruins of Zimbabwe, which – like the Pears' soap advert – thus places a Black African figure in the foreground. Students judge the Queen's likely ethnicity; she is definitely not a Black woman, and this is vital to the colonial regime, as the white colonialists attributed Great Zimbabwe's ruins to many different non-Black societies, including positing a Middle Eastern Queen of Sheba. Students then watch clips from Wheeler and Gates, and draw up a comparison chart between the two interpretations, highlighting Wheeler's description of the ruins as 'mysterious' and 'strange' and a comment from a white archaeologist that the buildings were not 'planned – they just grew', unlike the ordinary houses of European societies. This is contrasted with Gates's positive comment about the engineering feat of the Africans in building with such great stones, and the references Gates makes to the inappropriate interpretations of earlier Europeans. The agency of Black people is affirmed in this final film through the Black film-maker and Black archaeologist.

Lessons 3: How does Timbuktu have a reputation for learning and mystery?	*Summary:* The lesson sets up the contrast between the longstanding reputation of Timbuktu as a remote city of danger and mystery and the

relatively recent resurrection of a reputation for scholarly activity through its early manuscripts and ancient university. The students are confronted with both aspects and asked to come up with their own questions. This is the prelude to the overall enquiry question.

Activities include: An odd-one-out exercise that features Pitcairn Island, Cape Horn, Yamal in Siberia and Timbuktu. All of them are in some sense at the 'end of the earth' except Timbuktu, yet the latter has the strongest association with the term. Hunter Ellis's television clip then confirms the mystery idea with its dramatic soundtrack and editing. A more sober exercise considering Thabo Mbeki's visit in 2001 and his comments on the manuscripts sets up the alternative interpretation. Students can consider which of these views was more likely to be held by Hegel, connecting the idea of interpretations of Africa with this depth study of Timbuktu. Students produce their own questions on a separate sheet and table, which they will use to record and assess their own learning and progress through the enquiry. They finally write down the overall Timbuktu enquiry question.

Lesson 4: What were the origins of the city of Timbuktu?

Summary: The lesson explores historian Alexio Motsi's claim that the manuscripts were 'more than gold' and connects this to the first two lessons on impoverished interpretations of African history. It challenges the students' understanding of what 'treasures' might be. The importance of gold is then explored with respect to the trading city of Timbuktu, and in considering the idea that it is the place where 'camel meets canoe'. The arrival of Islam in West Africa is also connected to trade, and students should notice that the arrival of Islam into the region is not connected with conquest, unlike the spread of Islam in parts of North Africa and the Middle East. The political rulers of West African polities, from the empire of Ghana in the eleventh century onwards, saw the value of having Muslims in their cities, not just for the traded goods they brought, but also the benefit of having literate men who would record details of the empire's business.

Activities include: Students' own questions play a key part at the start of the lesson, and the record sheet will be continually in use, as the class topic(s) answers the particular question they had posed. A trade map is important, and it is essential that they understand the importance of salt as well as gold, establishing its role in preserving food and explaining why it is called 'white gold'. The sheet introduces the arrival of Islam into West Africa, through the trade route from the east.

Lesson 5: What connects learning and the religion of Islam in the manuscripts at Timbuktu?

Summary: The idea is to give students time to explore Islam and the manuscripts. Using images of two of the manuscripts, the students begin by speculating what might be in them, and how the content might be connected to Muslim religious practice. The last part of the lesson considers the initial connections between literacy and trade, and then the emergence of a trade in manuscripts themselves.

Activities include: A video clip concerning the astrolabe and the importance of Muslim prayers introduces students to the religion; astronomy was important not only for telling the time by the sun and stars, but also for telling the direction of Mecca, which Muslims face during prayers. A second manuscript is about oral hygiene and toothpaste. Photographs of men praying show the importance of clean breath for worshippers' comfort. Some students may have seen the natural toothbrush before – it is a piece of a tree, where the bark has been scraped back to reveal the natural fibres of the tree, which act as a brush for cleaning the teeth.

Lesson 6: How was Timbuktu ruled in the Middle Ages?

Summary: The idea is to examine the special way in which Timbuktu was ruled, and how political decision-making was placed in the hands of the city's scholars. We apply the term 'epistocracy' to the city, and then consider how those scholars attempted to combine Islamic traditions with local African culture, to produce a 'tolerant Islam', in contrast with the current media fixation on the 'intolerant Muslim threat'. Finally, the importance of education for an epistocracy is considered, and the Sankore university system is explained. There is a sense of both democracy and epistocracy at work here, with everyone participating in education early on, and the wisest scholars then becoming the rulers. The graduation ceremony with the special turban illustrates the blending of Islamic and African cultures.

Activities include: Students begin by reading a short description of Timbuktu from Leo Africanus in the sixteenth century, and consider an image that shows no city walls. They then look at four kinds of government – democracy, gerontocracy, autocracy and epistocracy – matching four jumbled definitions. The idea of Timbuktu as an epistocracy is then explained. Students watch a clip about the development of wisdom in Timbuktu through the blending of Islam and African culture, and the tolerant approach of the scholars who ruled the city. Students finish by watching a short clip about the graduation ceremony.

<table>
<tr><td>

Lesson 7: What was the impact of the Empire of Mali on Timbuktu?

</td><td>

Summary: This is quite a sophisticated examination of how the two political systems of the autocracy of the Mansa of Mali coexisted with the epistocracy

</td></tr>
</table>

of Timbuktu, and hence preserved the unique nature of the city's position. The two political systems are compared, showing how the strengths of one compensated for the weaknesses of the other. Kanka Musa's haj (pilgrimage to Mecca) in 1324 shows the ostentation and devotion of the autocrat, and emphasizes his respect for learning and Timbuktu's uniqueness. However, the growing reputation of his empire drew attention to Timbuktu, and the disadvantages of this appear in the Cresques map of 1375.

Activities include: The first section involves group discussions comparing the systems of autocracy and epistocracy, and then exploring the idea of them complementing each other in Mali and Timbuktu. Students then watch a clip about Kanka Musa's haj; they discuss the significance of his wealth and reputation and how it continues to show the blending of Islamic and African cultures. Then consider the short- and long-term impacts of the episode for the city, including the publicity given by the Cresques map.

Lesson 8: Why is Ahmed Baba remembered so fondly by the citizens of Timbuktu?

Summary: The decline and fall of Timbuktu is the context for the story of Ahmed Baba, who represents a heroic figure in contemporary Timbuktu with its Ahmed Baba Institute. The reasons for the decline of Timbuktu are presented in a conventional manner, looking at economic, political and religious factors. The enquiry was not designed to give a complete history of Timbuktu, so the period of French colonial rule is not explained, although the presence of the French is clear from the language used by the Africans in all the clips. The emphasis is on the example of the city as a centre of African civilization and learning through many centuries, although one largely unknown to Western eyes.

Activities include: Students watch a video about Ahmed Baba, and consider how he defended his city and people without actually fighting back physically. The importance of preserving his Black African identity should be highlighted, as well as the importance of his city's learning and the insistence on including in his name the epithet *As-Sudani*, meaning 'Black man'. They consider the questions: In what ways did Ahmed Baba defend Timbuktu? Why did he surrender to the Moroccans and what were the consequences? Students finish by discussing: What did Ahmed Baba mean by 'The ink of the scholar is more precious than the blood of the martyr'? How did he show the meaning of this in his life? The final outcome piece for the enquiry is a presentation of this quote in the form of a poster-manuscript.

Transforming the learning and teaching of African history

Historiographical discussions have traditionally been introduced into the classroom at an advanced level, at university or in the last years of school. Debates on contrasting interpretations could be considered not only intellectually demanding, but also rather dull for young adolescents. Yet our explorations of Black history, which has been manipulated and distorted by Western historians and teachers, necessitate discussions about historical interpretations. This African history enquiry hinged on challenging the stereotypical notions of the 'Dark Continent'. We found that, far from disengaging our students from their history lessons, seeking justice for the history of Africa and Timbuktu energized them and sustained their involvement throughout the enquiry. We believe that a key inspiration was the figure of Georg Wilhelm Friedrich Hegel. Establishing an antagonist the students could rail against proved to be highly effective. The history classroom became a contestable space, in which young people eager to express their independence could legitimately voice opposition while doing justice to history.

This enquiry was taught recently at a large Church of England girls' school in South London where over half the students are from African-Caribbean backgrounds. The Year 9 students (14-year-olds) were outraged at the words of Hegel they heard in the first lesson: 'Africa is not a historical part of the world; it is a continent cloaked in darkness: a land enveloped in the black colour of night.' Their teacher was able to capture their outrage and channel it into motivating them in the subsequent five lessons. Hegel was brought back at several points in the enquiry process. As the students considered the evidence of African civilizations, such as Zimbabwe and Timbuktu, they were invited to speculate about Hegel's response. The idea of setting up an antagonist also determined the final assessment: students wrote individual replies to Hegel.

The concept of a personal antagonist appeared to heighten the involvement of students in their history lessons, and the device was to prove valuable in other work we did. In the enquiry about Robert F. Williams and the African American Civil Rights Movement (discussed in Chapter 4), historian Adam Fairclough became something of an antagonist, since it was the omission of Williams from his book that inspired the students to search for a more valid interpretation.

Even though academic scholarship has long rejected the calumnies of Trevor-Roper and Hegel, misconceptions about Africa are still widely held.

We have a similar task to the one Thomas Browne had some four hundred years ago in trying to reveal the hidden histories of African civilization. But in some ways our task is harder, because the myths of barbarism are now so well-entrenched. Moreover, the Timbuktu enquiry was working not only with those stubborn myths but also with the misconceptions of Islam that have proliferated in the first decades of the twenty-first century. We selected Timbuktu as the focus of an African history enquiry because it would challenge the Western narratives of both Africa and Islam, and the feedback from students indicates that it has the potential to transform both. In a North London co-educational, multiracial comprehensive school, Tavistock High, three students in a Year 8 class gave the following responses in their evaluation of how they felt the Africa-Timbuktu enquiry had done justice to history:

> They taught us Africa have [*sic*] history, so it should not be known as a 'place with a dark history' and now people have learned about it, they can talk about Africa and back up their reasons.
>
> (Year 8 student, Tavistock High)

> Thank you for showing us another way to view Africa. Not just that they were slaves but they had religions and wrote in Arabic. Also it showed us that there is always two ways to view anything.
>
> (Year 8 student, Tavistock High)

> Justice to history means to me that we are unlocking the hidden secrets of Africa that many people had kept quiet for centuries.
>
> (Year 8 student, Tavistock High)

We can see a dynamic sense of learning here; the first student talks about a process of spreading the new knowledge gained by the students about Africa, and taking that forward into new discussions with others about the ways Africa has developed. It seemed the students had been locked in the 'dark' view of African history themselves, even though many of them were of direct African heritage.

The students had also been aware of the pejorative stereotypes of Muslims, although they were clear that the media was primarily responsible for this. The students' own views about Islam appeared more balanced before the enquiry, and about a third of the class were practising Muslims. One student commented:

It did justice because it would change how some people view Muslims, not just saying all Muslims are terrorists as you see the news portrays them, but realizing they are nice, smart, civilized people, not suicide bombers.

(Year 8 student, Tavistock High)

It is encouraging that many of the students thought this historical enquiry had the potential to change people's beliefs and attitudes to Africa and to Islam. They thought this would result from the unreservedly positive light the enquiry threw on the development of the highly civilized and literate society at Timbuktu. Students at a Catholic boys' comprehensive in North London debated the meaning of the quote from Ahmed Baba that featured in lesson six of the enquiry – 'The ink of the scholar is more precious than the blood of the martyr' – and one student put forward the idea that while the martyr's blood achieved something at the time it was shed, this would not last in the way that a scholar's writings could.

This work on Africa lies at the heart of doing justice to Black history in secondary schools. Contemporary media portrayals of the continent are still largely negative. Students need to confront the historical antecedents of these views in the distorted historiography that developed after the seventeenth century. Despite Thomas Browne's pioneering work and warnings, there are 'Vulgar Errors' about Africans to tackle still in 2016 that he highlighted in 1646. We hope that our 'interruption of the psyche' about the early history of Africa and its many civilizations inspires students and teachers to radically rethink populist interpretations. And engaging with African history as a shared heritage for people of the continent and the diaspora offers an opportunity for greater unity among Black people. If the enquiry on the history and manuscripts of Timbuktu can play even a small part in that, it would be, as Alexio Motsi says in our first lesson, 'more than finding gold'.

Chapter 4

Forgotten stories in the African American Civil Rights Movement

African American Civil Rights

In *A Tempest*, his 1992 adaptation of Shakespeare's play, anti-colonial Black thinker Aimé Césaire grappled with the difficulties facing the decolonized people of Africa, especially the philosophical challenges facing those involved in the African American Civil Rights Movement. In Césaire's version the character of Ariel, still the loyal agent and captive servant of Prospero, the tyrannical patriarch, is a thinly veiled portrayal of Martin Luther King Jr, an intelligent being working with Prospero in the hope of securing his freedom. Caliban, the dangerous and unruly beast, equally under Prospero's dominance, makes little attempt to do Prospero's bidding. He vehemently asserts that he doesn't trust Prospero's conscience since Prospero is 'A man who only feels something when he's wiped someone out' (Césaire, 1992: 23). The rhetoric echoes Malcolm X's fiery speeches denouncing non-violent resistance and accommodationism. The play ends with Ariel gaining his freedom, but not in the dignified way he sought, while Caliban escapes (Fei, 2007).

Césaire's *A Tempest* is similar to the mainstream approach to teaching the Civil Rights Movement in its focus on these two figureheads of the struggle. Martin and Malcolm have become the two most recognizable African-American icons of the twentieth century, but the popular understanding of them rests on caricatures and sound-bites. Césaire's subtle analysis of the Civil Rights Movement is rarely given exposure in the history classroom: it seems to be neither wholly critical nor entirely complimentary towards the approach of either Martin or Malcolm; both Ariel and Caliban have honourable intentions and seem to act with integrity according to their circumstance. Césaire's Ariel and Caliban never resort to violence to win their liberty from Prospero; the pain comes from Ariel's dishonourable success in winning freedom by satisfying Prospero at the expense of Caliban, who later exults in his more noble escape.

The same could be said of the Civil Rights Movement in the mid-1960s. Neither Martin nor Malcolm advocated the use of violence, but towards the end of the decade it was Malcolm's philosophy that inspired the Black Power movement. These radical activists considered the early gains of the Movement to be symbolic, feeling that they had failed to address the poverty and unemployment facing most African Americans. Martin Luther King Jr had in fact campaigned against poverty and unemployment; the assassin's bullet cut short his move away from complete accommodationism. Yet some of the lessons we observed and most of the textbooks we studied fell into the trap of polarizing the two leaders: Martin the pacifist prophet of non-violence as against Malcolm the dangerous alternative, a villain or at best an anti-hero.

Last year one of Robin's trainee teachers was asked to plan a lesson and came to him for advice, unsure whether what she had been asked to do was appropriate. The lesson in question was part of an enquiry on the African American Civil Rights Movement and she had already planned and taught a lesson on Martin Luther King Jr and the Christian inspiration for his non-violent approach. The problem arose when she was asked to contrast that lesson with another that linked Malcolm X to the Islamic concept of jihad. She felt uncomfortable about comparing the two men in this way and came to Robin because she didn't understand the complexities of Malcolm X's relationship with Islam. Robin suggested that she explore the positive transformative effect of Islam on Malcolm X's life, and particularly how he renounced the racist views of the Nation of Islam when he embraced orthodox Islam after his pilgrimage to Mecca in 1964.

This example illustrates a problem that undermines the validity of many classroom history lessons. The desire to make lessons interesting and 'relevant' can lead teachers to presentism. The department wrongly understood jihad in the sense in which it is commonly used today, probably because Malcolm X was a Muslim and has been characterized as a violent hate preacher who opposed the peaceful Christian reverend Martin Luther King Jr. This false binary is easily accepted since it fits with the populist portrayals of these men and the tensions between the two religions today. But the Civil Rights Movement was complex. It is this complexity that makes it so worthy of study in the classroom. It does not ruin a 'good story' if, like James Cone (1992) in *Martin & Malcolm & America: A dream or a nightmare,* one argues that instead of being implacable foes, the men complemented one another and shared the same social goals, and that the gulf between their political views narrowed towards the end of their lives. Clayborne Carson (2005) bemoans how even now their respective political evolutions still remain poorly understood, because they challenge those who prefer a simplistic narrative of heroes or villains.

Another challenge facing educators is the structure of examination specifications in the UK and in the US. The Movement is framed as a struggle that began with the Montgomery Bus Boycott and ended with King's assassination. One exam board in the UK has gone a step further, ending the bulk of one A-Level unit on African-American history in 1968 and beginning its final section only in 2004 with Barack Obama's journey to the White House. The missing decades of the seventies, eighties and nineties are full of relevant complexities; the change in emphasis from political to economic equality remains a challenge for many teachers. The all-too-obvious problems of ghetto poverty, race-related crime and enduring racial tensions demand thorough exploration (Verney, 2006), even if one believes the Civil Rights Movement ceased to be relevant after 1968.

One possible reason for this academic omission may be that this material does not supplement the hopeful narrative that we now live in a 'post-racial' society. The importance placed on citizenship education in the US and UK suggests a political imperative in the propagation of curricula that support national and community cohesion. Britain has indeed taken some significant strides in anti-racism over the last 25 years. The Macpherson Report (1999) identified institutional racism within the Metropolitan Police Force and all public services, and eight years later the Strand Report (Strand, 2007) confirmed that schools were institutionally racist. The work undertaken by government and other authorities to address the findings of these reports has arguably led to a belief that racism no longer poses a major problem in British society, alongside a fear of raising issues surrounding race lest one be labelled a racist.

The statutory obligation to be respectful of all ethnic and cultural groups (Equality Act, 2010), combined with the fear of causing offence, has led many teachers to choose the 'safest' option when teaching topics that deal with the issue of race. They set up the topic of civil rights to create a false binary between racial integration and Black nationalism. Martin Luther King Jr and Malcolm X recognized the different positions they occupied even when they began to see room for significant cooperation, but students are asked to choose between the two. Young Black people seeking social justice are still torn between racial integration and racial separation. Recent studies show that Black people do not benefit from the 'storehouse of positive assumptions reserved for their White and Asian counterparts' (Ford and Bobb, 2011: 13). Black males in particular are the victims of unfair treatment in the classroom and are disproportionately excluded from school (New Policy Institute, 1998). They constitute only 1 per cent of students in higher education, whereas Black girls account for 16 per cent (Sutherland, 2006). Such trends have remained consistent across decades. The reality of race in society confronts Black men and boys at every turn, since success in most societies depends to an extent on routes of compliance and assimilation that are not open to them. Robert Jensen (2005), in his book on the issue of white privilege, explains the endurance of racism in modern America. Despite efforts such as affirmative action in the US and legislation in the UK, Black people still face economic and social barriers wherever white privilege is a fact of life.

Fear of the 'angry black man' is still a root cause of discrimination in schools, the workplace and civic life (Sutherland, 2006). The 'good negro/ dangerous negro' binary still dominates the study of the African American Civil Rights Movement. A doctoral scholar at Queen Mary University in London, Rob Waters, who has researched the impact of stories of the Civil Rights Movement broadcast on British television in the 1960s and 70s (Waters, 2013), found that many British people used this medium to frame their nascent ideas about race in Britain; television programmes often contrasted Stokely Carmichael with Martin Luther King Jr. A similar pattern is evident in the school curriculum today. Are we teaching that there are 'safe' Black people, like Dr King, and 'dangerous' ones like Malcolm X? Is this shaping the contemporary view of race relations? If so, a heavy burden falls on classroom teachers to take a lead by offering all students the opportunity to explore race in a meaningful way. If the Civil Rights Movement is taught, it should be done in a balanced and accurate way. It is the extraordinary diversity of those involved and the complexities of their contributions that make it an episode of history with which students can engage deeply, whatever their ethnic background.

Historical perspective: Robert Franklin Williams and Dr Martin Luther King: a Bourdieusian analysis

The traditional history of the African American Civil Rights Movement, spanning the years from the Brown Decision against segregated schooling in 1954 to the death of the movement's pre-eminent leader Dr Martin Luther King Jr in 1968, is repeatedly portrayed as a major turning point in American history and part of the fulfilment of the nation's destiny as a land of freedom. The ideal of the American Dream, associated with notions of liberty and equality, was seen to have been brutally assailed by the assassination of Dr King (Kelly, 1968), while his life and the achievements of the Civil Rights Acts of 1964 and 1965, which he played a major part in securing, were deemed to have given African Americans unprecedented access to that dream. Dr King had aligned himself with that vision in August 1963, when he spoke at the Lincoln Memorial during the rally of the March on Washington for Jobs and Freedom, giving his iconic 'I Have a Dream' speech. King portrayed images of an integrated and just society, and the speech was used from then on to depict an idyllic post-racial society, where race and 'color' would cease to matter. Forty years later, many Americans (and others worldwide) consider that vision of a post-racial American Dream to be embodied in Barack Obama's election as the first African-American US president (Atwater, 2007).

Dr King has a hagiographic historical reputation that makes him instantly recognizable across the globe, particularly where people look for benign role-models that can assuage fears of angry Black men demanding rights with menaces. Dr King is not without his detractors, but white people who want to assault him find it easier to deplore his philanderering, rather than attack his message of integration (Dyson, 2000). For Black people, however, Dr King is more likely to be criticized for his racial politics and the struggles for Black equality. From the strident criticisms articulated by Malcolm X from the late 1950s onwards, Dr King has been condemned as an accommodationist 'Uncle Tom' by some militant Black activists who grew impatient with his non-violent creed. King grew up in Atlanta in the Deep South of the US, and led successful civil rights campaigns in other Southern towns and cities that were dominated by the Jim Crow system, which King worked to dismantle. His critics came mainly from northern states and major urban ghetto areas, where it was not legal frameworks of *de jure* segregation that subjected African Americans to grave depredations and indignities but de facto segregation and discrimination. Many urban working-class youths could not relate to the respectable, Southern, middle-class Black preacher. However, the South did offer also an alternative hero whom such African Americans could admire.

Robert Franklin Williams was the leader of a local group of the National Association for the Advancement of Colored People (NAACP) in the small town of Monroe, North Carolina. Williams was seen as uncompromising and fearless in his call to resist white violence by armed self-defence (see Figure 4.1), and he refused to adopt the unequivocal commitment to non-violence that Dr King advocated, although he saw the value of non-violent resistance in some situations (Williams, 2013). However, Williams is conspicuously absent from the conventional narratives of African American Civil Rights history (Crosby, 2002). Authors who wanted a foil for the saintly Dr King already had one in Malcolm X, who fitted other convenient binaries, being northern, working-class, non-Christian and a convicted felon. Besides, Rob Williams never courted the limelight, nor did he feature in events after 1961, when he was exiled until 1969. Since the years of exile saw the apogee of the Movement, his sidelining would not seem to be a significant error.

Yet when Robert F. Williams died in 1996, Rosa Parks, the most prominent woman in the Civil Rights pantheon, proclaimed at the eulogy she gave at his funeral that 'The work he did should go down in history and never be forgotten' (Parks, quoted in Tyson, 1999: 3). Parks chose to honour a man who would probably be presented as an enemy of the type of leadership for which she herself was remembered in the Montgomery Bus Boycott. So, although the lives of Martin Luther King Jr and Robert Franklin Williams do show marked differences, there might be fundamental values and principles that they shared. Rosa Parks was able to associate herself with both men. Furthermore, recent studies of her life suggest that, if we grasp a nuanced and authentic idea of her activism, she can be seen as surprisingly close to Robert F. Williams (Theoharis, 2009).

Figure 4.1: Robert F. Williams and a group of his followers in Monroe, North Carolina

King and Williams were born quite near to each other, and a few years apart: King in 1929, in Atlanta, Georgia, and Williams in 1925, in Monroe, North Carolina, less than five hours' drive away. Although contemporaries, they inhabited quite different worlds. Timothy Tyson (1999) opens his pioneering account of Williams with a story of how he witnessed brutal racial violence in Monroe when he was eleven years old. He saw an African-American woman being dragged by her hair across the streets to the jailhouse by a local police officer, and was stunned by the way the local Black men watched the spectacle silently with their heads bowed. The police officer's son, Jesse Helms, later became a US Senator. Robert repeated this story in public throughout his life, and it was clearly a spur to his activism. On the other hand, when Martin Luther King was questioned in a 1961 television interview about his experiences of Southern racism when he was young (*Face to Face*, 1961), the only example he offered was being slapped by a white woman for accidentally stepping on her foot in a department store when he was eight years old. The young King certainly was aware of the violent actions of the Ku Klux Klan and other white supremacists, but he seemed somewhat shielded from the naked aggression that had horrified the young Robert Williams.

Although both inhabited the Deep South, where segregation and racism were deeply rooted, King and Williams were from very different backgrounds, and this affected their later leadership. Bourdieu's constructs of *habitus* and *field* (Maton, 2014) can help us in comparing the two. Bourdieu defines habitus as 'that which one has acquired, but which has become durably incorporated in the body in the form of permanent dispositions … it refers to something historical, linked to individual history' (ibid., 55). King was from a church leadership family and went from an Atlanta high school to the prestigious, historically black Morehouse College, and eventually to Boston for doctoral studies in theology, returning to the South in 1954 as pastor of Dexter Avenue Baptist Church in Montgomery. King's spiritual and intellectual life was thus very different from that of Williams, the son of a skilled railroad worker. Williams too went north, to work in Detroit at the age of seventeen, but was drafted into the American army towards the end of the Second World War and returned south to Monroe in 1946. So, although both were acutely aware of the Southern way of life, with its harshly enforced racial divide and mores, their responses were framed by different values and attitudes; each had his own habitus.

Bourdieu emphasized that it was not habitus alone that determined a person's practice; the field in which one operates is equally important. Karl Maton (2014) expresses the interaction between them:

> Where we are in life at any one moment is the result of numberless events in the past that have shaped our path. We are faced at any moment with a variety of possible forks in that path, or choices of action and beliefs. This range of choices depends on our current context (the position we occupy in a particular social field), but at the same time which of these choices are visible to us and which we do not see as possible is the result of our past journey, for our experiences have helped shape our vision.
>
> (Maton, 2014: 51)

When he was confronted with white violence in Monroe, Williams never for a moment thought of 'turning the other cheek' and responding non-violently. He regarded armed self-defence as the sensible entitlement of any American citizen, in the same way that the white citizens of his town did. Williams had spent three years in colleges in the north during the early 1950s, and he regularly composed poetry; arming himself was based on pragmatism, not machismo. King, on the other hand, had been drawn into the thinking of Gandhi and Thoreau through his university studies, and developed a philosophy that led him to urge his followers from the pulpits of the Black churches in Montgomery to respond non-violently to aggression.

In their late twenties, neither Williams nor King sought positions of leadership in the field of political activism. Both were fathers of young children and exploring ideas about life and citizenship, but they were thrust forward in the absence of other suitable contenders. King was selected as leader of the Montgomery Improvement Association when the bus boycott started late in 1955 because he was a neutral choice against the older, competitive African-American pastors in the town, and Williams became head of the NAACP in Monroe in 1956 because its six members were about to disband the group he had only just joined. Both men encountered situations that marked a turning-point in the development of their leadership, thrusting them into an unsought limelight.

In January 1956, King's wife and child were threatened by a bomb attack at their parsonage home in the early days of the bus boycott, and he sought strength and guidance from his God in what became known as the 'kitchen experience' (Garrow, 1987). In the middle of the night, King received yet another threatening phone call, and a sense of isolation and danger drew him into an intimate encounter with God in prayer. His leadership position was greatly strengthened by his epiphany, and after the successful resolution of the boycott, King became the leader in 1957 of what was to be one of the pivotal groups in the Civil Rights Movement, the

Southern Christian Leadership Conference (SCLC). Williams, meanwhile, took up a cause that was less significant in the national struggle than the Montgomery campaign, but did mark a success in overcoming the racist intransigence of the Southern system. In the 'Kissing Case' of 1958, two young boys in Monroe, aged 10 and 8, were sent to reform school for over ten years for kissing a young white girl in a playful game after school one day. Much more highly charged than the question of segregated seating on buses, this case carried the perilous combination of racial and sexual taboos, and Williams mounted a major campaign, on an international scale, to bring pressure on the governor to intervene. The young boys were released after four months' incarceration.

The year after the Kissing Case, King and Williams were pitted against each other in the pages of a magazine called *Liberation*. They never met in person, and perhaps a live debate would have tempered the advantage Dr King had in written argument, especially when the journal had Williams write first, with King responding to his ideas in his own time. Williams had acknowledged the importance of adopting King's non-violent protests in certain circumstances. King had identified three positions African Americans could adopt in the face of white oppression: non-violence, self-defence or violent offensives. Unfortunately, the media portrayed the two men's positions as totally opposed, because King insisted on placing Williams in the category of violence, when he was advocating self-defence (Tyson, 1999). King appeared reluctant to acknowledge the strengths of Williams's position, but Williams was more magnanimous.

The print debate was read with interest by James Forman, a young man who played a leading role in the Student Non-violent Co-ordinating Committee (SNCC) in the 1960s, and he considered there to be no dichotomy between the two positions, despite the way people were interpreting them (Forman, 1997). James had experience of a number of centres in Northern and Southern states, and he said, 'I knew that too much noise was being made by his [Williams's] critics and not enough attention paid to the conditions that made self-defense necessary for Black people in the United States' (ibid.: 159). The leaders went on to produce books about the application of their philosophies; King's publications included *Stride Toward Freedom: The Montgomery story* (1958), which stressed the successful impact of non-violent protest. Williams wrote only one book, titled *Negroes With Guns* (2013; first published 1962).

In the later years of campaigning, King recognized that he had to be more flexible about armed protection when challenging Southern fields (in the Bourdieusian sense). In 1966, in Mississippi, King took the advice of SNCC's leader Stokely Carmichael stating that it would be foolhardy to pursue a non-violent march in that state without protection, so King allowed the Deacons for Defense and Justice to follow the marchers through Mississippi, but discreetly, at the edge of the crowd of protesters (Carmichael, 2004). The more experienced King could defer to the judgements of others when he was in an alien field and acknowledge the wisdom of the alternative habitus. On that march Carmichael encouraged the famed 'Black Power' chant, with its connections to more assertive activism and the eschewing of total non-violence. By then Robert F. Williams was living in exile in China, having had to flee the USA in 1961 after facing trumped-up charges of kidnapping following a disturbance in Monroe. He came home in 1969, a year after King's assassination. Williams lived until 1996, and Rosa Parks said how pleased she was to attend the funeral of an activist who had lived a long life and avoided enemy bullets.

Parks, like her fellow Montgomery leader, King, also never met Robert Franklin Williams, yet she powerfully endorsed his legacy in her eulogy. Why? Possibly her own habitus had developed in the forty years since her own legendary achievement in the Civil Rights Movement. When the Montgomery Bus Boycott ended, Rosa Parks and her husband moved to Detroit in the North after both were fired from their jobs during the boycott. Parks became involved in numerous campaigns for justice for African Americans, and supported their right to self-defence. As she said, 'I could never think in terms of accepting physical abuse without some form of retaliation if possible' (Park, quoted in Theoharis, 2009: 116). None of these details appear in the traditional narrative of the Civil Rights Movement, and they reveal the crudeness of the binaries that it presents about civil rights and Black Power: Martin Luther King Jr versus Malcolm X; non-violence versus violence. Robert F. Williams has been left out of this narrative, not only because his impact appeared to be modest and the traditional interpretation already has its threatening antagonist in Malcolm, but also, perhaps, because the alternative stance of this Southern militant might not have been as unusual as established liberals and integrationists would like it to be.

Developing the African American Civil Rights enquiry

The African American Civil Rights Movement is one of the most widely taught topics in British history education. Both of us have seen how it is taught in the classroom. We wanted to develop an enquiry that offered a fresh approach to the topic and to structure a learning experience for students that would free them to grapple with the complexity and diversity of the

Movement. By the age of fourteen many students have some knowledge of the Movement, either through classroom teaching or films and television. So our challenge was to construct an enquiry that harnessed their awareness of the traditional narrative to uncover the various ideologies and personalities that we believe make studying the Civil Rights Movement so worthwhile. We especially wanted to challenge the almost Manichean message of the conventional narrative in which King is the messianic protagonist fighting Southern segregationists and extremists within the Movement. We were determined to find a way of sustaining higher-level thinking by weaving the key events into a narrative that allowed opportunities for meaningful dialogue about substantive concepts such as Christian pacifism, armed self-defence, masculinity and the 'southern way of life'. The activist we felt could be the focus of an enquiry that best explored these concepts was Robert F. Williams.

The planning process began with a skim through a popular book on the Civil Rights Movement, *Better Day Coming* by Adam Fairclough (2001). We were surprised to find that Williams's name was not in the index. This highly respected account of the Civil Rights Movement from 1890 to 2000 made no mention of Williams, despite Timothy Tyson's substantial biography of Williams published in 1999. Our fleeting surprise morphed into what Dewey described as a period of 'felt difficulty'. As we continued our research on Williams, Fairclough's omission of him kept a hold on our thoughts until we decided that the enquiry we were developing for teaching in the classroom should reflect the challenges we encountered in our research. Tyson's biography helped us form the enquiry question; to emphasize Williams's significance, Tyson quotes Rosa Parks saying at Williams's funeral that his work 'should go down in history and never be forgotten'. Parks's strong defence of Williams's legacy and Fairclough's exclusion combined to form the key question: 'Why has Robert F. Williams been forgotten?'

That neither of us could offer a good answer confirmed that this was indeed the sort of question that could expose the process of constructing warranted historical accounts so that students could arrive at their own understandings of the past through an enquiry-based approach. For the lessons to reflect our own process of learning as historians, we would begin with Rosa Parks's words. In the traditional narrative she is presented as a Black woman who had been pushed too far by the discrimination of the South and who set the Civil Rights struggle in motion with her quiet defiance on a bus one day. Most textbooks and resources fail to mention the deliberation behind the celebrated moment, her training in passive resistance, her role in the NAACP and its selection of Parks to challenge the segregation on Montgomery's buses (Theoharis, 2009). We knew the students would respect her at once and therefore recognize her authority in commending Williams. When we introduced Williams through a photograph showing him heavily armed and smoking a cigar, we were hoping the students would lose what Kierkegaard (1992) calls 'their sense of balance' and begin to question their own assumptions about Rosa Parks and also about armed Black men.

The second lesson had to give students some contextual understanding of life for African Americans in the South. For students to make valid judgements about Williams's actions and philosophy, they needed to understand his environment. We also aimed to demystify the Ku Klux Klan by exploring the ubiquity of their presence in towns like Monroe and allowing students to conclude for themselves that they were agents of white hegemony who used force to maintain white power in the South. This lesson reinforced the dual nature of the enquiry, by which students learn the key events and developments of the traditional narrative while they try to answer the enquiry question, which, although presented through the story of a relatively obscure figure, helps them to enquire more deeply into the major issues surrounding life and protest in the Deep South.

The tragic story of David 'Fuzzy' Simpson and Hanover Thompson was a powerful example of white power in the South. These African-American boys, aged 8 and 10, were sentenced to juvenile detention until the age of twenty for the crime of playing a game of kiss-chase with a white girl. The boys were eventually released after Robert F. Williams became a 'one-man press campaign' that shamed the Governor of North Carolina into releasing them. The story of Emmett Till, the young boy from Chicago who was brutally beaten to death in 1955 for the crime of whistling at a white woman, might appear to be a better example for exploring the taboos around so-called miscegenation and the fears of racial inter-mixing in the South. But Till was murdered by segregationists acting outside the law, whereas Simpson and Thompson were sentenced according to the laws of their state. This aspect more than anything conveyed the shocking, brutal power of Jim Crow.

Originally, we did not plan to use Bourdieu's concept of habitus to develop students' understanding of life in Monroe and the South. Abdul had been teaching an A-Level sociology class about Bourdieu's theories and during his next lesson with the Year 9 history class he spoke about the significance of social environments in determining people's thoughts and actions. The concept of habitus in relation to the Southern way of life enabled them to question and reach complex understandings about the realities of racial segregation.

We often used photographs at the start of lessons in the enquiry, to 'interrupt the psyche'. Students would offer their responses to sources that seemed to contradict their understanding of the enquiry themes. A photo used at the beginning of the third lesson showed a sign in Memphis, Tennessee stating in bold letters 'NO WHITE PEOPLE ALLOWED IN ZOO TODAY' (see Figure 4.2). The students were asked to explain how far this demonstrated that life was good for African Americans in Memphis. Many students thought at first that it was a misprint since they had become so used to seeing signs that proclaimed the exclusion of 'colored' people. Eventually they recognized it as another example of the determination of Southern states to enforce segregation.

Figure 4.2: Overton Park Zoo, Memphis, Tennessee, in the 1950s (image © Ernest C. Withers, reproduced by kind permission)

This strongly dialogic starter on the nature of segregation proved an ideal introduction to the beginning of the student-led sit-in movement in Greensboro, North Carolina. Here the focus was on the level of hostility the Greensboro students encountered in their protest and on comparing this to the likely reaction they would have received had they attempted this in the smaller but more violent town of Monroe, where Klan rallies attracted up to 15,000 participants. The habitus in which Williams operated was illustrated by a story from his youth that Williams repeated countless times to defend his position on the necessity of armed self-defence. We decided that the best way to convey the message would be to read it out from Timothy Tyson's exposition:

> For one black boy in Monroe, North Carolina, the earth first shook on a Saturday morning in 1936. Standing on the sidewalk on Main Street, Robert Franklin Williams witnessed the battering of an African American woman by a white policeman.
>
> The policeman, Jesse Alexander Helms, an admirer recalled, 'had the sharpest shoe in town and he didn't mind using it.' The police officer's son, Sen. Jesse Helms, remembered 'Big Jesse' as 'a six foot, two-hundred pound gorilla. When he said, "Smile," I smiled.'
>
> Eleven-year-old Robert Williams watched in terror as Big Jesse flattened the black woman with his fist and then arrested her. Years later, Williams described the scene: Helms 'dragged her off to the nearby jailhouse, her dress up over her head, the same way that a cave man would club and drag his sexual prey.' He recalled 'her tortured screams as her flesh was ground away from the friction of the concrete.'
>
> The memory of this violent spectacle and of the laughter of white bystanders haunted Williams. Perhaps the way that African American men on the street responded was even more deeply troubling. 'The emasculated black men hung their heads in shame and hurried silently from the cruelly bizarre sight,' Williams recalled.
>
> (Tyson, 1999: 1–2)

The impact of this story on the students was evident and the young Williams's shock at the response of the emasculated African-American men added to the complexity of Black resistance. Many students expressed surprise at Williams's later restraint in his attempts to peacefully desegregate the municipal swimming pools even though he was shot at.

The fourth lesson began by highlighting the treatment of those who tried to use peaceful methods of direct action to challenge segregation in the South. An ambiguous image of a man pouring unidentified liquid into a swimming pool in which people, black and white, were screaming, reminded students how brutal it could be: the liquid was sulphuric acid.

The primary objective of the lesson was to introduce Martin Luther King Jr, the most vocal proponent of peaceful protest, and to get students to question King's unflinching commitment to non-violent direct action in the South and his total opposition to the concept of armed self-defence. In 1961 King was challenged by Robert F. Williams to a platform debate on the issue, but rejected the offer in favour of a debate on the pages of *Liberation* magazine. We gave students enough material to help them replicate this debate, explaining their own views about King's approach and the situation in Monroe.

The penultimate lesson introduced the national Freedom Rides of 1961, the final major aspect of the traditional narrative. Earlier lessons had dwelt on the exceptional violence of Monroe even by the standards of the South, and also the fear of miscegenation that was a pillar of Jim Crow laws. The Freedom Riders, a multi-racial group of idealistic and energetic activists drawn from all over the country, epitomized the greatest fears of Southern segregationists. We show a televised interview in this lesson, featuring a white British activist, Constance Lever, who had joined the Freedom Riders. She recalled the hostility directed at white participants when they reached Monroe: they were constantly called race traitors and 'nigger lovers', and many were spat on and beaten. Lever speaks of Williams's honesty and says she perceived him to be a man of strong convictions (Tyson, 1999). This gives students another angle on his significance, but also an understanding that distinctions between him and more steadfastly non-violent activists such as the Freedom Riders were due largely to the different environments they inhabited.

The arrival of the Freedom Riders in Monroe and the violence they provoked from the segregationists prompted an angry response from the black residents of Monroe. Things reached boiling point when a white couple took a shortcut through a Black neighbourhood and suddenly found themselves surrounded by an angry mob who appeared ready to kill them. They sought refuge in Williams's house, which he granted. But he refused to escort them out of it. They eventually managed to leave unharmed, but reported Williams to the police, claiming he had kidnapped them. The subsequent media coverage focused almost exclusively on the testimony of the white woman, Mrs Stegall, but not that of her husband. This prompted discussions about the nature of racial and gender intersectionality in the South. This example, along with the story of the Black woman who had been beaten by policeman Jesse Helms, showed the mixed-ability group of 14-year-olds the role of masculinity in the maintenance of white power in the South. And it also explained why Williams believed that the only way to counter it was by asserting a black masculinity in which owning firearms affirmed their status as men (Estes, 2005).

The final lesson of the enquiry explicitly addressed the enquiry question, and so focused on the period after Williams escaped to Cuba. The students had some ideas by then about why he had been forgotten, helped by the timeline they had kept that displayed the traditional narrative and the events of Williams's life either side of the date line representing his exile. They could see therefore that his time in Cuba meant he was away while the Southern struggle grew from a modest group of Black students demonstrating peacefully at one lunch counter to the largest movement for racial reform and civil rights in the twentieth century (Marable, 1991). By this point in the enquiry many students agreed with Rosa Parks that Williams 'should go down in history and never be forgotten', but they still needed to understand why he did not receive recognition for his contribution to the movement.

The discussions for this lesson focused mostly on the growth of the Black Power movement, which was heavily influenced by Malcolm X and other proponents of armed self-defence such as Williams (Estes, 2005). The final detailed answer to the enquiry question incorporated much of the traditional narrative, citing people who had given their views on Williams and his approach. The aim is for students to focus explicitly on the nature of Williams's significance, and to consider how significance can come in the form of quiet influence for a new generation of activists, as well as highly visible activities such as internationally broadcast speeches. The students should be aware that interpretations play a major role in deciding what is or isn't significant. Williams may well have been forgotten because his message was one that many who clung to Martin Luther King Jr's dream would find dangerous and subversive.

Table 4.1 Outline of the six-lesson enquiry on Robert F. Williams and the Civil Rights Movement

Why has Robert F. Williams been forgotten?

Lesson 1: Who was Robert F. Williams?

Summary: The enquiry begins by introducing the Civil Rights Movement through an 'odd-one-out' activity that places Robert F. Williams alongside well-known figures from the 1950s and 60s such as Martin Luther King Jr, Malcolm X and John F. Kennedy. The students are now suitably grounded in the historical context, so can begin to explore the potential significance of the least-known figure, Robert F. Williams. Students are challenged throughout this lesson to question significance by exploring the validity of different interpretations. The quote from Rosa Parks, stating at his funeral in 1996 that Robert F. Williams 'should go down in history and not be forgotten', is introduced. Possible explanations are presented, chiefly through a video of Williams and a group of African-American men posing with a range of firearms; the clip is narrated by his biographer Timothy Tyson. The lesson ends with the students being asked to propose the enquiry question: why has Robert F. Williams been forgotten?

Activities include: Completing an odd-one-out exercise designed to generate an open, dialogic approach to the learning, followed by further discussion about the validity of comments drawn from Rosa Parks's eulogy for Robert F. Williams. A video explaining Parks's role in the Bus Boycott in Montgomery supplements student's knowledge and ability to offer a reasoned response. Considering the index page of Fairclough's *Better Day Coming* further develops their understanding of the link between significance and interpretations. The students are then in a position to make their own tentative judgements about Robert F. Williams, but they also recognize the need to learn more about him and his world. This impels them to generate the enquiry question themselves.

| Lesson 2: How did the Southern way of life affect the people of Monroe, NC? | *Summary:* This lesson explores the 'habitus' of the South and the realities of what was referred to as the Southern way of life. |

The Ku Klux Klan and their dangerous and pervasive influence in the South are contrasted with the NAACP's ever more successful legal challenges to the system of segregation they fought so hard to preserve. Williams's career in the NAACP is explored through his role in the acquittal of two boys who had been imprisoned for allegedly kissing a white girl.

Activities include: Studying a map of the USA, which highlights the divide between the Jim Crow South and the North. Students examine the number of active KKK members in Monroe and how this would have affected the Black people there. Two videos are shown; one explains the nature of the 1954 Brown decision (a step forward, albeit in a legal sense) and the unjust incarceration of two Black children, aged 8 and 10, for kissing a white girl. Discussion of the video focuses on the severity of the punishment and the significance of the 'colour line' in the case.

| Lessons 3: What was protesting like in Monroe, NC? | *Summary:* The mid-point of the enquiry allows students to delve deeper into life in the Jim Crow South. Examples of segregation are presented followed by a |

study of the student lunch counter sit-ins, also in North Carolina but some miles north of Williams's hometown of Monroe. Sources that describe the protest movement they inspired are compared with the efforts of the NAACP, with Williams as its leader, attempting to non-violently desegregate the swimming pools in Monroe by attempting 'wade-ins'. The murderously violent reaction inflicted on the protesters becomes the focus of the lesson. This lesson also introduces a story Williams often told about witnessing a brutal police attack on an innocent Black woman when he was a child. This powerful story, coupled with the evidence about violent responses to non-violent civil disobedience, gives students a greater understanding of the link between Williams's habitus and his advocacy of armed self-defence.

Activities include: Studying an image from the mid-1950s of a sign outside a zoo in Mississippi stating 'NO WHITE PEOPLE ALLOWED IN ZOO TODAY': a different way to present segregation in the South. This is a prelude to a short video, which gives some background about attempts at forcing desegregation in the South. The teacher reads from Williams's description of a racist attack he witnessed as a child in Monroe. The students then watch a video that further outlines his beliefs, except now they are being asked to compare Williams's approach with what was happening in the traditional narrative of the Movement: could there be sit-ins in Monroe?

Lesson 4: Why did Martin Luther King Jr disagree with Williams's approach to desegregation?	*Summary:* This lesson introduces Martin Luther King Jr as a key figure of the enquiry; his appeal in places like Monroe, NC is investigated.

King's unequivocal commitment in 1961 to pacifism is demonstrated via a video interview. This is used to prompt students to explore why King might have been seen as a more acceptable figurehead for the African American Civil Rights Movement by moderate segregationists. King's approach is directly contrasted with Williams's through a written debate, echoing the nature of the public debate between the two in 1960.

Activities include: Student discussion and analysis of a photographic source displaying the cruelty perpetuated by staunch segregationists. This is followed by watching a 1961 BBC interview about Martin Luther King Jr's approach and answering questions on this topic. The lesson concludes with an essay answering the following question: *Explain why Dr King and R. F. Williams disagreed about the best way for African Americans to challenge segregation in the Civil Rights Movement. You should refer to the situation in Monroe, NC, in your answer.*

Lesson 5: How did Robert F. Williams end up on the FBI's most wanted list?

Summary: The Freedom Ride movement alluded to in previous lessons is explored in greater depth. The key question for students to explore at the beginning of the lesson is whether such methods of protest would be successful in Monroe. Another video is used to show what happened when the Freedom Riders passed through Monroe, with the hospitality but not the full support of Robert F. Williams. The discussion continues with a final video that explains Williams's role in saving from a Black mob a stranded white couple who later claimed to police and the media that he kidnapped them. This led Williams to flee Monroe and obtain political asylum in Cuba. The students are now in a position to explore the nature of racism across the United States, at a time when the national media and the FBI presented Williams as a dangerous criminal and accused him of fomenting unrest even while the evidence proved that his actions in this instance were designed to maintain order.

Activities include: A number of edited videos are used in this lesson to allow students to link the national Freedom Rides movement with the repercussions for Williams of their visit to Monroe. The lesson concludes with students writing a radio broadcast as though given by Williams from his sanctuary in Cuba, in which he explains to Americans why he should not be labelled a criminal and why the charges against him should be dropped. Students are given some transcripts from his radio station in Cuba, Radio Free Dixie, to give them a sense of his anger and quiet eloquence.

Lesson 6: Why has Robert F. Williams been forgotten?

Summary: The final lesson presents a number of reasons why Robert F. Williams has been forgotten, to add to the reasons students have already discovered, such as his period of exile in Cuba. Students can now learn about the development of the Civil Rights Movement and the growth of Black Nationalist movements, all of which supported and promoted the concept of armed self-defence as necessary in the fight for equality. More subtle reasons for Williams's exclusion from the mainstream narrative of the Civil Rights Movement are also considered, such as his humble, down-to-earth manner and his reluctance to engage in self-promotion.

Activities include: Students explore the impact of Malcolm X and the later radicalization of the SNCC, and the emergence of the Black Panther Party for Self-Defence. Students record the views of Williams's contemporaries and their opinions of his impact before creating a display for a Civil Rights museum that includes Williams, along with other key figures, in a manner that best represents their view of Williams's significance. In the final task the students write a detailed response to the enquiry question: *Why has Robert F. Williams been forgotten?*

Transforming the learning and teaching of the African American Civil Rights Movement

In a research discussion about the impact of the Robert F. Williams enquiry at Milburn School, a multicultural, coeducational comprehensive in North London, one of the students, Malaika, explained why she felt she had gained so much from her participation in the enquiry:

> We learn so much when our teacher lets us explore different answers together, that's how we get a discussion started ... when we listen to everybody's answers we become more conscious of what we've said and it makes it stick in your memory.
>
> (Malaika, Milburn School student)

When asked what was the most memorable moment of the enquiry she hesitated before referring to a discussion about the photo used at the beginning of lesson four:

> I think he wanted everybody to think about it, and get everybody's opinions, and like that we were learning rather than having what we were told and just having a normal lesson, we had the time and space to get discussion started.
>
> (Malaika, Milburn School student)

Dewey (1933), Burbules (1993) and Montaigne (2004) are among the philosophers of education who argue that learning can occur only amongst equals. It cannot be based on authority because genuine dialogue is its core activity. Learning to do justice to history in the classroom should promote independent thought and critical reflection. The process of dialogue is critical to this, since it is the basis for the inclusive, invitational approach to learning that Malaika believed allowed her to think about her learning in proximity to others. In response to a question about the significance of the enquiry question in history, another student in the class said that the question was more important than the answer because it was open to multiple responses and spawned many other questions that aided his understanding.

Every lesson in the Robert F. Williams enquiry was designed with the aim of promoting student-led dialogue. Although the students knew the teacher had some idea what the answer to the question would be, they felt empowered when entrusted with creating their own interpretations based on the evidence. Many students in the group spoke about the liberating feeling of putting their hand up knowing that they could offer a response that would be used and developed by their classmates. Much of this was stimulated by their reaction to the first lesson. Presenting Adam Fairclough's omission of Williams along with Rosa Parks's eulogy at Williams's funeral created the 'felt difficulty' that enthused students in their pursuit of a deeper understanding of the Civil Rights Movement.

The integration of the traditional master narrative alongside the story of Williams's role in the movement contributed greatly to students' understanding, and they remarked on how much knowledge they had absorbed. One month after their lessons on Williams the students at Milburn School demonstrated remarkably detailed recollection of specific conversations about how his habitus influenced his ideology. The intellectual dimensions of the enquiry had certainly had an impact on their learning. Their use of the terms 'habitus' and 'field' gave them a demonstrably greater ability to express themselves. Such words and concepts allowed them to feel comfortable expressing themselves as intellectuals.

In February 2015 we taught this enquiry to a group of final year matric (university entrance) students in Pietermaritzburg in South Africa. The classroom for the twelve students during this week was the living room of a large beach house near Durban, which created an atmosphere quite different to their regular formal school classroom. Sipho, one of the students, explained how important it was for him to understand the respective backgrounds of Robert F. Williams and Martin Luther King Jr before he could come to a judgement about whether Williams was justified in his advocacy of armed self-defence. In a two-minute section of an interview we conducted with him, Sipho used the term 'habitus' four times to explain why he believed Williams had been unfairly characterized as a 'violent crusader'; he clearly relished demonstrating his intelligence and recognized how the complex concept opened up a valuable way for him to explore the challenges Williams faced in Monroe.

Interviews with the younger London pupils and the older South African students showed that the enquiry had a profound impact on both. The impact on the South African students was more complex and even emotional. They had grown up in a country that had only two decades earlier dismantled a social system not unlike that of America's Deep South in the time of Robert F. Williams. The influential power of environment over people's behaviour and conduct was recognizable for many of them, although the events discussed happened before the students' time. They had also studied aspects of the Civil Rights Movement prior to learning about Robert F. Williams. Sipho and his classmate Nkosi explained how looking at the Movement through this 'obscure' figure gave them the confidence to criticize Martin Luther King Jr and other key figures:

> We had always been taught that Martin Luther King was an angel, that he never made any mistakes but now we know we only got part of the story. Learning about Robert F. Williams helped us to understand Martin Luther King better ... he was wrong not to speak out against Vietnam and to have secret deals with Lyndon B. Johnson.
>
> (Sipho, matric student)

They welcomed the complexity that the enquiry added to their prior understanding of the Civil Rights Movement and recognized that the history they enjoyed most was controversial and contested.

Not all enquiries into a period of history should focus on a single individual, but the use of one personal story within a greater movement that drove change can have a strong impact on young people's view of history. The combination of the master-narrative and the hidden individual history can be especially motivating for students because it has the power to harness their innate sense of justice and fairness. This sustains the in-depth exploration of the significance of individuals within history and can engender sophisticated judgements about the inherent subjectivity of historical interpretations.

Chapter 5

Teaching the history of apartheid in South Africa

Race and apartheid in the history classroom

Few topics in school history resonate with the theme of 'justice' with greater force than South Africa in the twentieth century, and the rise and fall of apartheid. The white supremacist regime in South Africa stands out as the epitome of injustice in the modern age. Few children today have not heard of Nelson Mandela. Doing justice to this history may seem easy, and many schools in England and elsewhere use Mandela's *Long Walk to Freedom* and his merciful post-apartheid benevolence as a single, uncomplicated narrative to support the worthy goals of social cohesion and equality. The white people of South Africa who established the system of apartheid, which translates as 'separateness' but means structural inequality, are taken to represent the ruthless greed and prejudice that underpin racism in the modern world.

This South African history appears to have no significant 'strange' dimension that need trouble history teachers; all the necessary history is part of the 'familiar' (Wineburg, 2001). However, there is an important difference between finding justice *in* history and doing justice *to* history. Nelson Mandela may exemplify justice in his actions, but a narrow focus on him does not do justice to the complexities of 50 years of constant socio-economic, political and religious upheaval in Africa's most ethnically diverse country. As Mandela himself declared: 'It is not the Kings and Generals that make history but the masses of the people' (Mandela, quoted in Stevens, 2012). So there are histories of people who resisted apartheid, including white South Africans, which have been obscured, overshadowed by Mandela and other iconic figures such as Steve Biko. Teachers have to confront and investigate the 'strange' past if their students are to learn that social change is hardly ever achieved by single triumphal acts.

At the heart of the history of apartheid South Africa is the concept of race. Doing justice to the historical and contemporary features of 'race' as a concept and a determining force is challenging and complex. There has been much talk in recent years of a 'post-racial' society, particularly following the end of apartheid and Mandela's presidency in 1994, and then the election of Barack Obama as the first Black president of the United States in 2008 (Sugrue, 2010). There have indeed been major advances at the turn of the twenty-first century in breaking down barriers of race and people's racial perceptions, and the overturning of apartheid is seen as a milestone among those achievements. Besides new legal and constitutional support for the equality of racial groups in many countries, Black people have shown greater confidence in challenging inequalities.

There are, however, people who still assume that race is a matter of biology, and are challenged by the idea that it is a political construct (Allen, 2012). Some people prefer to deny its existence and adopt what is termed a 'colour-blind' approach. This risks ignoring the vast impact the construct has had over centuries, and continues to have. Race remains a real and sensitive issue, partly because of the catastrophes of the last millennium, principally the transatlantic slave trade and the Holocaust, and because of its power to hurt and discriminate. This can make it a difficult matter for people to engage and wrestle with; it is easier to accept the dominant discourse, whether that is a negative, exclusive, racialized view of competition between groups, or a superficially benign acceptance that racism is wrong and people should all live together in harmony.

Our approach is to acknowledge that race is constructed and to explicitly consider its historical and contemporary impact. An enquiry on apartheid allows for explicit teaching about race, but we realized that it could have a considerable impact on the sensibilities of those involved. We taught the enquiry in South Africa as well as the UK, so had many issues to consider. The sense of discomfort that many people in the 'new' South Africa feel about their 'grim past' is palpable. The weight of justice within South Africa's history-making can prompt even the most skilled statesman to suggest it be avoided; even Mandela occasionally called on South Africans to 'forget the past', although he did say the opposite, too (Stolten, 2007). There is a consensus that the post-1994 era was not a fruitful one for the development of history in South Africa and the subject struggled to establish itself in the reformed school curriculum of 2005 (Dubow, 2007). The South African Education Minister Kadar Asmal, who was a significant figure in the rescuing of school history as a curriculum subject, said in 2004:

> We need to build an inclusive memory where the heroes and heroines of the past belong not only to certain sectors, but to us all ... Memory is identity, and we cannot have a divided identity.
>
> (Asmal, quoted in Stolten, 2007: 44)

It is generally accepted that one of the important purposes of school history is to help to develop young people's sense of identity within their nation and community (Barton and Levstik, 2004). But that becomes problematic when the racial divisions of the past seem to condemn one group of students to be identified as perpetrators.

We thought the hidden histories of the apartheid years might be better known in South Africa itself, but we discovered inhibitions and challenges that appear to have closed down explorations of apartheid history in South African schools. In the summer of 2012 we arrived at a small multiracial school in Pietermaritzburg, with the intention of teaching recent South African history to its students, who come from a range of ethnic backgrounds. The school had a unique lineage. It was established as a multiracial primary school in the late 1980s when apartheid was still in force. The school's founders believed that their Christian faith impelled them to embrace white and Black South Africans as equals. By the time we arrived, the school had operated a secondary department for more than a decade, although it remained very small and had fewer than 300 students. History was taught throughout the school, following the national state syllabuses, which included the story of apartheid, and its demise, twice in the secondary school cycle, as well as touching on the subject in primary school lessons. While we were there, one of the white girls of British heritage, Anne, spoke in an assembly about the trauma that came with learning about apartheid in her primary school class: girls were in tears and friendships in peril as racial lines were suddenly drawn. Their nation's racial history appeared to be something the young people preferred to avoid in the interests of social cohesion.

The students at the Pietermaritzburg school were very good-natured and polite with adults and generally with one another; the ethos of the school was stunning in its warmth and camaraderie. Yet the students almost always sat in their own racial groups in class. Anne, the student who had spoken in assembly, told us that it was simply easier for her to get to know the other white girls well, even though she was quite happy to mix with other racial groups. Avoiding any discussion of race and the commitment to a multiracial society appeared to be insufficient to overcome latent anxieties about mixing. In England our students tend to socialize and work more often in diverse racial groups, of which there are many in metropolitan centres. However, there are still barriers for Black people in England, especially to high-status professions and positions, and subtle everyday racism persists, sometimes in the form of incidents termed 'micro-aggressions'. Nevertheless, there is little discussion of race in English schools, and both teachers and students are generally guarded in their references to the issue (Maylor, 2010). The opportunity to openly discuss the construction of race and its historical development within our apartheid enquiry could be significant not only for fashioning a post-apartheid South Africa, but also for grappling with what might become a 'post-racial' world everywhere.

Historical perspective: the significance of Nelson Mandela and Sharpeville

'If one person can change the perspective of everyone, there's something wrong with society.' These are the words of Ezekiel, a 13-year-old in a history class in a London school that had been learning about apartheid by studying some of its less well-known opponents. The discussion took place after their enquiry into apartheid South Africa, and only days after the death of Nelson Mandela. They had all been asked how they felt when watching some of the media coverage of Mandela's funeral. Ezekiel went on to describe a heated debate he had with his parents as they watched the television coverage. As images of the massacre at Sharpeville were flashed onto the screen Ezekiel conveyed his bemusement to his parents: Mandela had nothing to do with Sharpeville. His parents refused to believe him. They could not appreciate that this iconic episode in the apartheid saga did not include its greatest figure.

The inauguration of Nelson Mandela as president in 1994 was undoubtedly a turning point in the history of modern South Africa. It brought an end to 46 years of National Party rule. The subsequent dismantling of the racist social system that party had statutorily instituted raised difficult questions for the post-apartheid state. How would it begin to reverse the enormous inequalities endured by the Black majority? Before the election even took place the only question, it seemed, was how any change could be achieved without civil strife breaking out, with threats made by political groups on either side of the racial divide. Nelson Mandela referred to the peaceful elections as 'a small miracle'. It is an apt phrase, because many believe that without his leadership fragmentation and violence would have been inevitable.

Mandela's insistence on moving forward and forgiving his enemies has allowed South Africans of all races to create a 'resistance to redemption' narrative that has at its heart Nelson Mandela as an almost messianic figure, whose legacy is beyond reproach. Such a narrative inevitably excludes significant events and people in the apartheid era. Mandela himself, in his first speech on release from Victor Verster Prison, stressed to the amassed crowd that he '[stood] before them not as a prophet but as a servant of the people' (Mandela, 1990) before going on, at length, to list all the movements and organizations that had helped secure the progress his release promised. Although his release was widely proclaimed as a move away from the past, the spectre of past injustices loomed large over the event.

On the day of his release South African state news television, still operating under strict censorship, had the difficult job of presenting the event as a victory for the National Party. Their chief reporter for the event was one Hendrik Verwoerd – not the architect of the apartheid state but his grandson. In many ways Prime Minister (and later President) Hendrik Verwoerd was the principal antagonist in the Mandela redemptive story. Although D.F. Malan is credited with establishing the apartheid state after the 1948 election, it was Verwoerd who gave shape to the sketchy notion of apartheid. Even with the victory of the National Party in 1948 it was by no means inevitable that the system we know as apartheid would take hold in South Africa. That it did is largely down to the personal conviction and will of Hendrik Verwoerd the elder. Editor of the Afrikaans newspaper Die Transvaler, he became recognized as a leading Afrikaner intellectual whilst holding a position at the premier Afrikaner seat of learning, Stellenbosch University, as a professor of Sociology. Through his two roles he developed an intimate understanding of Afrikaner society and sought solutions to the problems it faced. His first great cause was the issue of white poverty, but once appointed Native Affairs Minister – controlling the vast majority of Black South Africans – his story would forever be bound with what is referred to as the 'high tide' of apartheid. One of his first major acts was to dismantle the Native Representation Council, because 'it was useless for the Bantu people to get involved in the general principles of higher politics' (Dubow, 2014: 65). Verwoerd went on, as head of state, to turn his white supremacist ideology into the workable philosophy we can recognize as apartheid – although Verwoerd was keen to translate it as 'separate development'.

The resistance the state faced from Black Africans was at its weakest in the 1960s under Verwoerd's stewardship. This was partly due to unprecedented national economic growth that increased employment for Black Africans to its highest point ever, although wages, in real terms, didn't increase; neither were there any advances towards economic parity between whites and Blacks. Another reason why resistance from Black Africans declined under Verwoerd was the relentless suppression of any viable opposition to his vision for South Africa. The year 1961 saw the conclusion of the Treason Trial of the leaders of the major organizations that had met at Kliptown near Johannesburg in 1955 to create a 'Freedom Charter'. By the time it ended, after five years, the fact that all the defendants – amongst them the leader of the African National Congress, Albert Luthuli – were acquitted was deemed 'irrelevant' by many involved in the resistance. In the eyes of the world the outcome of this trial had already been superseded by one single event in 1960: the Sharpeville massacre. This killing of peaceful protesters by the police exposed the brutal reality of enforced racial segregation that Verwoerd had so desperately tried to present as even-handed 'separate development'.

Protest in the 1950s had focused mainly on issues of employment or living conditions. When, in 1958, the activist Robert Sobukwe left the African National Congress (ANC) to form the Pan-African Congress (PAC) he made it clear that their protests would be directed against the hated Pass books (known to many Black Africans as the *dompas* or 'stupid pass') that non-whites had to carry at all times and present on demand to police. The passes dictated where you could live and work, and even what work you could do, and allowed the white authorities to keep close control over the Black majority. Therefore many believed the pass laws were the cornerstone of the apartheid system. Sobukwe and the PAC leadership, like Gandhi before and Martin Luther King Jr after, decided to challenge unjust policies by openly defying them and demanding to be sent to prison. The ambition to 'fill the jails' meant that protests would have to be persistent and involve large numbers. The PAC's first major public protest was arranged for 21 March 1960. Sobukwe was wary of how the authorities would respond to his calls for Blacks to leave their passes at home and demand to be arrested, so he wrote the police chief a letter outlining the intentions of the demonstration and stressed that they were fundamentally peaceful (Pogrund, 2006). His letter received no reply. We can only speculate about what went through the minds of the white police officers stationed at Sharpeville Police Station as the crowd grew in number and demanded to be arrested. The police responded by firing into the crowd, killing 69 unarmed demonstrators, many of them shot in the back as they fled.

Sharpeville was a signal to Black Africans that peaceful demonstration alone would not bring an end to apartheid. To the wider world it was the impetus for the process of political and economic isolation of South Africa that reached its fullest expression in the late 1980s as South Africa sank to the status of a pariah nation. To a few whites Sharpeville made clear that they could not both support the policies of the governing National Party and also hold the moral high ground. It certainly proved to be a turning point in the life of Beyers Naudé, a white minister in the pro-apartheid Dutch Reformed Church (DRC), one of the many people whom Mandela thanked, days after his release, for their contribution to the movement. What is most exceptional about Beyers Naudé was how he publicly sacrificed the privilege of being an Afrikaner of considerable influence within the DRC in order to distance himself from the obvious brutality being committed to maintain this privilege.

Naudé's emergence after 1963 as a vociferous critic of the regime did not prompt many in his position to follow him, and this limited his immediate significance within anti-apartheid resistance movements. The growing dissent among prominent churchmen towards government policy grew in the immediate aftermath of Sharpeville but was quickly stifled. The speed with which the government and also the Broederbond, an Afrikaner secret society of which Beyers Naudé's father had been a founding member, managed to achieve this suppression belies a lack of real conviction on the part of those early dissenters. Many Afrikaners were swayed into supporting apartheid because it was presented as the only way to guarantee white supremacy and prosperity. Supporters of the regime controlled dissent from the whites, and especially the Afrikaner community, by turning critics into outcasts. Naudé's own prevarication over declaring himself an opponent to the regime had at its heart a fear of the backlash and subsequent isolation that his family would face if he did so. The organization Naudé helped to establish after Sharpeville, the Christian Institute, like other white-led anti-apartheid organizations was slow to realize that despite their privileged position as whites, they would not be the significant instrument of change. The Black Consciousness movement, along with the increasing maturity of Black resistance organizations such as the ANC and the PAC, instead would serve as the instruments of change in South Africa, and they were supported from outside (Dubow, 2014).

One reason for the disproportionate attention to Mandela in the story of modern South Africa could be that the political activities of some of the nation's most influential Black activists were too often cut short by their untimely deaths. Sobukwe's death at age 53, upon early release from prison in 1978, came as a relief for the apartheid regime. After the judge handed down to Sobukwe an initial three-year sentence for incitement in the wake of Sharpeville, the government hurriedly justified his continued extra-judicial detention under what became termed the 'Sobukwe clause'. Besides this, Sobukwe's insistence on working only with groups who were not consciously or sub-consciously safeguarding existing privilege meant his views were frequently misrepresented as 'anti-white' rather than Africanist, a term he deemed flexible enough to someday encompass whites. To the regime Sobukwe was a terrifyingly dangerous opponent, whose advocacy and use of 'positive action' could eventually lead to majority rule and the end of white privilege. In his 2006 biography of Sobukwe, *How Can Man Die Better?*, Benjamin Pogrund describes a leader who, even as he lay dying as a result of protracted mistreatment, still spoke in conciliatory and forgiving tones about those who had sanctioned his mistreatment. Many believed at the time that Sobukwe's death had removed the one figure who could unify the Blacks towards the goal of a peaceful transition to majority rule.

Though Sobukwe and Mandela were at one point only a few metres apart on Robben Island, the two were never allowed to speak to each other. Mandela's patience and longevity allowed him to become the unifying leader the nation needed. A victim of Verwoerd's increasing suppression of dissent throughout the 1960s, Mandela is now universally admired for his ability to overcome the legacy of the past. But in our eagerness to herald the great man's notable achievements, we must not ignore the sacrifices of other significant leaders. Perhaps there was a time when to deeply explore the contributions made by a range of figures to the anti-apartheid movement would have proved fractious for an emerging nation, but with the 'Rainbow Nation' having passed its fourth presidential election it may be time to construct a new, more complex national narrative, one that can make space for figures such as Robert Sobukwe and Beyers Naudé.

Developing the Beyers Naudé enquiry

It may be easier for two teachers from London than South Africans to undertake the task of teaching lessons on apartheid. We could distance ourselves from the legacies and implications that surround South African teachers, both white and Black. South African textbooks cover the details of the history the teachers were supposed to teach, but they don't really probe the conceptual challenges, particularly those surrounding the notion of 'race'. We were to teach an enquiry on the history of apartheid to classes in South African Grades 9 and 11 (15- and 17-year-olds). Our classes would be racially diverse, and we imagined that the selection of material for the enquiry would be fundamental in encouraging students, whatever their ethnicity, to pursue their history studies with an essential 'felt difficulty'. Could that felt difficulty be the same for different racial groups, given the grim past? Any focus on apartheid could give a different meaning of 'difficulty' to the students depending on their ethnicity. We wanted to ensure that 'difficulty' meant Dewey's perplexity, not deep discomfort throughout our lessons (Dewey, 1933). Although Dewey believed that some discomfort was often valuable in the process of changing a person's understanding through enquiry, it should only be momentary discomfort, and enquiry should quickly establish a lasting sense of achievement.

When we began preparing for the enquiry, our own knowledge of South African history was limited to the familiar figures in the conflict between Blacks and whites: Mandela, Luthuli and Biko, versus Verwoerd, Malan and Botha; we didn't know of anyone who would fulfil Kadar Asmal's call for more varied heroes. But while we were searching for video clips to resource the lessons, we discovered an extract from an interview in 1983 with a white South African. Its title on YouTube was 'Beyers Naudé in interview', and this set us off on research about this Afrikaner pastor. The recording showed Naudé in a very emotional state, and it was easy to sympathize with his plight. A prominent white South African pastor, immersed in the world of white supremacy upheld by his church, he had nonetheless rejected the doctrine of apartheid. We had found a historical figure with a perplexing circumstance – his forced resignation from his church in 1963 – that could be a source of enquiry and identification for all our South African students, as well as doing justice to history. Here was a narrative about a white South African that disturbed the common stereotype of racist oppressors.

So we put Beyers Naudé at the centre of our enquiry, and set the enquiry question as: 'Why did Beyers Naudé break rank from his church in 1963?' We used an edited section of the video that described only his resignation and departure from the ministry to begin the first lesson, giving no indication that Naudé's decisions related to apartheid and the Sharpeville massacre. The wording of the question was designed to build on the intrigue by using the phrase 'break rank', rather than the familiar 'leave', and we spent time explaining that idiom with the students. The following lessons explored how and why church ministers in South Africa would have supported a discriminatory regime, and looked at the particular strand of Black resistance developed by Robert Sobukwe, culminating in the Sharpeville protest. No more was said about Naudé until the last lesson when the full video clip was shown, which revealed the connection between Sharpeville and his resignation.

How, then, was Beyers Naudé significant? The question of historical significance is related not only to the importance of something in its particular time and place, but also to its subsequent impact. Significance should also be considered in relation to historical interpretations. Naudé's significance in the apartheid story is drawn from his power to bring a more inclusive dimension to a very important aspect of Black history. The lessons focused chiefly on the roles of Verwoerd and Sobukwe, but it would be Naudé's presence at the heart of the enquiry question that challenged the

usual historical interpretations. Teaching an enquiry that is centred on
Naudé rather than Mandela could involve students in the pressing task of
exploring South Africa's complex racial past.

There was little academic writing on Beyers Naudé for us to explore,
but we were able to gather information that suggested he would have had
a strong connection to the fabric of apartheid: his father had been one
of the leaders of the Broederbond, an organization that provided a lot
of the intellectual preparation for apartheid, and his sociology teacher at
Stellenbosch University was Hendrik Verwoerd, the future prime minister.
We had to speculate a good deal about Naudé's early understanding of
apartheid. We assumed he would have absorbed Verwoerd's ideas about
'separate development' unquestioningly (Giliomee, 2012), since it was the
official position of the Dutch Reformed Church in which he served. The
DRC preached white supremacy over the 'lower nations' of Black Africans.
We found an excellent video that afforded us primary sources in the form
of television interviews undertaken by an American journalist with some
minor figures in the Afrikaner establishment in 1957 (CBGP News, 2015).
The interviewer, Mr McCutcheon, asked probing questions of these pillars of
the new segregationist system, implying criticism of this white supremacist
regime. McCutcheon seemed dubious about the fairness of apartheid, but
he made no reference to the similar 'Jim Crow' system in the South of the
USA, and neither did his interviewees. The irony appeared lost at the time,
but it seems an obvious thought now.

We focused on two men. First was Domini (Minister) Burger of
the Dutch Reformed Church, who tried to justify the separation of God's
people into white churches and Black churches, and emphasized the notion
that both sides were happy with that arrangement. The other key figure was
Mr Prinsloo, a minor government minister, who described the white South
Africans with their separate civilization as a flower, comparing them to the
Black Africans, who were another kind of flower, with features he thought
valuable, such as the 'warmth of their sociable character'. Prinsloo declared
that the flowers should be allowed to blossom side by side in their own
space, but he failed to point out the glaring disparity between the fertility
of the soil for whites and the meagre weed-ridden scrubland for the Black
South Africans. Although the reasoning of Burger and Prinsloo would seem
unbelievable to our students, the interviews were intended to help them
understand how South African Christians like Naudé could square the
harsh oppressions of apartheid with their faith.

This work was followed by a study of Hendrik Verwoerd, shown in
a short televised clip, and in a powerful cartoon published in England that

showed him with his perfidious smile presenting a pretty flower labelled 'Separate Development' to the world, and concealing a dark thorny flower called 'Apartheid' behind his back (see Figure 5.1). This would give students the basis on which to analyse and explain the tensions inherent in the policy of apartheid, such as Verwoerd's notion of 'good neighbourliness', namely that 'good fences make good neighbours'.

Figure 5.1: A British cartoon of Verwoerd and the policy of Apartheid (image reproduced by kind permission of Leslie Illingworth/Solo Syndication)

Black African opposition to apartheid was the focus of the fourth and fifth lessons, with Robert Sobukwe the central figure, the unsung hero of the Sharpeville Massacre of 1960. He exemplified the dualities in accommodation and resistance of Black African peoples worldwide. We devoted some time to Sobukwe's background, and his immersion in white British South African culture, followed by a career in a white university, along with his proud African upbringing, which forged an implacable opposition to the newly imposed apartheid system. Sobukwe was especially incensed by the pass laws, which were to be the focus of the protests on 21 March 1960 at the township of Sharpeville and elsewhere. Sobukwe was the head of the Pan-African Congress, which advocated a more exclusively Black African approach than the nascent 'rainbow coalition' of Mandela's party, the African National Congress. PAC did not believe that white South Africans could contribute to the struggle against apartheid, since they would always have so much to lose if they agreed to end the structure of white supremacy. The culmination of the Sharpeville protest was shown through a short video clip at the end of the fifth lesson. This needed little discussion; the haunting voice of the narrator reporting that 'most of them were shot in the back' left the students to make the obvious inference and leave with something of the sense of profundity that must have hit Beyers Naudé when it happened in 1960. Some students may then start to understand why Naudé broke rank from his church: this was the focus of the final lesson.

What took him so long? That was the question that struck us when we noted the three-year gap before Naudé announced his decision to leave the DRC. We then found out about his Christian Institute and his attempts to build a multiracial organization, and learned of Verwoerd's demand that his former student make a choice between church/state and his conviction – which he did. The final lesson began with the full video of the 1983 interview, which concludes with Naudé's tearful recollection of the Sunday afternoon encounter between himself and his wife when they realized the momentousness of his exit from the church and community that had shaped their lives, and their dependence solely on God. The televised moment is guaranteed to move students and teachers alike, and to bring them closer to the emotional world of a historical actor in a way that rarely happens in school history.

As we discussed the planning of this lesson, we hit upon the notion that Sharpeville had proved a kind of moral searchlight for Beyers Naudé, and other people in South Africa and around the world, revealing something that had been lurking in the shadows. The analogy that came to mind was the impact of a prison searchlight revealing a long-plotted escape, and we produced a diagram for the PowerPoint presentation that showed the world of South Africa bounded by the prison-fence of racial construction. Within it was a visible sector labelled 'Separate Development/Vision of Future Equality/Flowering Civilizations', and the text explained: 'The fence of racial construction has led to an established routine of thoughts, behaviours and actions. Apartheid needed routines, like the pass laws, to avoid a lot of questioning. An ultimate level of routine would be a prison.' The next two slides revealed the contents of the dark part of the enclosed area: 'Rule by Force/Brutality/Separate Non-development' and the printed comment: 'The moral searchlight only realizes its full range of movement when faced with a paroxysm of violence, as at Sharpeville.' The final assessment task for the enquiry had to be closely connected to Beyers Naudé, although we would want students to acknowledge also the impact of Verwoerd and Sobukwe in particular on the whole narrative. We asked the students to write a version of Beyers Naudé's final sermon, making clear the impact on him of Sharpeville. The connection made in this final lesson with the pastor invariably motivates students to complete the assignment.

Table 5.1 Outline of the six-lesson enquiry on apartheid South Africa

Why did Beyers Naudé break rank with his church in 1963?

Lesson 1: Who was Beyers Naudé and what happened with him in 1963?	*Summary:* The interruption of the psyche and intrigue of the enquiry is central, and the felt difficulty is having sympathy for a white South

African, who gives an emotional account of an incident in his church in 1963. We begin in the first half of the lesson with speculation about what might have caused him to leave the church, and the students may decide that it could have something to do with the system of apartheid. The second part explores Naudé's background and the Afrikaners' ideology of apartheid.

Activities include: The lesson begins by listening to the (edited) video clip of Beyers Naudé. Key vocabulary is explored: integrity, unequivocal, apartheid, Hamitic myth, breaking rank (in the enquiry question). Once the enquiry question is set, the background to apartheid is explored through the background of the Afrikaner people, and Naudé's father in the Broederbond, the elite Afrikaner society that did so much to fashion an Afrikaner identity and culture through the mid-twentieth century.

Lesson 2: How far could apartheid be considered a Christian system?	*Summary:* Christianity and apartheid are examined in juxtaposition in this lesson. The notion of all people being equal is understood to be at the heart

of the Christian religion (as well as other faiths), so it may seem contradictory for the churches of South Africa to support apartheid. A church minister's attempt to justify the system is pitted against students' ideas about the Christian gospel message. The notion of 'separate development' is explored as an allegedly benevolent approach to race relations, akin to 'separate but equal' in the USA.

Activities include: Listening to a video of Domini Burger, a Dutch Reformed Church minister in 1957, considering the content and the manner of speaking. The idea of 'separate development' is introduced through an excerpt from the same American documentary from 1957: a government official called Mr Prinsloo gives his metaphor of the two flowering civilizations in Africa. Prinsloo's stereotypes of the jovial warm African character can again be critiqued. Students conclude by answering a question: *Explain how and why a Christian minister, like Rev. Naudé, could support the system of apartheid.*

| Lessons 3: How valid were Verwoerd's claims about 'separate development' under apartheid? | *Summary:* Students confront the ideas of the chief architect of apartheid, Hendrik Verwoerd, and consider the credibility and sincerity of his ideas about separate development and |

'good neighbourliness'. The nature of 'race' as a socio-political construct is key to the lesson, and students may be surprised that race is not valid in the biological sense. Critical views of Verwoerd are considered in two cartoons that focus on notions of duplicity in his racial policies (and those of others in the national government). The connection to Beyers Naudé is made through the information that Verwoerd was Naudé's sociology teacher at university.

Activities include: Video clips are used to convey the ideas of racial classification in the apartheid state, and to show Verwoerd speaking about 'separate development' and his concern that opponents have misrepresented apartheid. His body language, particularly his smile, can be evaluated from the clip and the cartoon. The metaphor of flowers in the British cartoon links nicely with Mr Prinsloo's comments.

| Lesson 4: Why was Robert Sobukwe an 'extraordinary Black African'? | *Summary:* Black Africans feature in the second half of the enquiry, and the latent power of the size of the Black population is conveyed |

through a cartoon. Then the example of Robert Sobukwe shows how the themes of accommodation and resistance appear, again, in the history of the Black experience. The sophisticated immersion of Sobukwe in Western literature and music is a challenge to the simplistic notions of Black African culture espoused by Mr Prinsloo. Sobukwe's resistance is also revealed, and the students speculate about his reception by the apartheid establishment.

Activities include: A British cartoon is explored that shows a giant Black African figure loosely tied down by a small group of white South Africans, in the style of Gulliver in Lilliput. A video clip then describes the early life and education of Sobukwe. His personal struggles under apartheid, as well as his appreciation of Western cultural forms, in literature and music, are considered as possibly 'extraordinary'. (Baroness Orczy, one of his favourite authors, wrote about the Scarlet Pimpernel, a spy in the French Revolution, and one of the nicknames for Nelson Mandela was the 'Black Pimpernel'.) Finally we realize that he was given a teaching post at the white University of the Witwatersrand.

Lesson 5: What was significant about what happened at Sharpeville on 21 March 1960?

Summary: Black African grievances under apartheid are exemplified by the pass laws, and students are shown how the Pan-African Congress planned to mount a protest against them. Sobukwe's role in the protest is considered, as is the idea of 'no bail' and evidence on how the protesters were trying to undermine apartheid by flooding the jails. The massacre at Sharpeville is the climax, and some students might speculate that this is what moved Beyers Naudé to protest.

Activities include: Video clips are used to convey the main narrative of the lesson, which builds to the climax of the massacre in 1960. Students can study Sobukwe's letter to the police chief beforehand, warning him that there might be trouble at the protest. Although his PAC followers would not be armed, Sobukwe felt the police might over-react. Students can debate who was responsible for the massacre at Sharpeville: was Sobukwe culpable because he could foresee the possibility of violence?

Lesson 6: Why did Sharpeville have such a dramatic impact on Beyers Naudé?

Summary: Beyers Naudé becomes the focus of the enquiry at the end: the full video clip from his interview reveals that it was Sharpeville that led to his break from the church, and the final section reveals the emotional impact on his family. The power of events and personal conflicts is strongly conveyed by this source. The metaphor of a searchlight is then used to show the impact of Sharpeville on Naudé, and on international observers at the time. The power of the 'fence of racial construction' on the psyche of white South Africans created a sense that apartheid was normal, and led these white South Africans to accept the notion of 'separate development'. The 'searchlight' of Sharpeville revealed the brutality and inequality lying at its heart, which helps to explain Naudé's inner turmoil after 1960. When the state refused to let him stay in the church and continue the alternative organization he had established, which was working for an integrated South Africa, he had to leave.

Activities include: The full interview clip is the basis for a long discussion of the key question: Why did Sharpeville have such a dramatic impact on Beyers Naudé? The rest of the lesson uses a diagram of the searchlight metaphor, gradually revealing the dark side of apartheid, from an initial view of the system as something benign. The final assessment activity asks the students to write their own version of Naudé's farewell sermon.

Transforming the learning and teaching of apartheid

The teaching of South African history can easily rely on an uncomplicated singular narrative. To focus solely on the ordeal and later magnanimity of Nelson Mandela is tempting for teachers who wish to teach their students that history education is a source of moral guidance. The belief that children need heroes is not in itself flawed, but to use history in that way can detract from its many other purposes. Young people often choose their own heroes (Barton and Levstik, 2004) and the imposition of heroic figures into the history syllabus can have unexpected outcomes. Christiaan, a Grade 9 history student at Maritzburg School, explained why he was not looking forward to our lessons on South African history:

> I was quite dreading, I've always dreaded South African history, especially the whole apartheid thing, but it wasn't as bad as I thought it would be ... I quite liked the whole aspect of taking the whole enquiry question. I enjoyed the fact that the whole structure of all the lessons was based around Beyers Naudé who was actually a white person who stood up against apartheid, because you get Nelson Mandela and all those people, and sometimes for me as a white South African, who is Afrikaner, it sometimes feels, it was nice to see that there were white people who also fought against apartheid.
>
> (Christiaan, Grade 9 student)

This comment surprised us. For one thing, Christiaan was a highly academic and motivated student, and had demonstrated this in history lessons we taught him the previous year. For another, he was an Afrikaner who had a good many black African friends. The reason for his 'dread', as he goes on to explain, was principally his belief that the lessons on apartheid would convey the simple story he had been taught before. Christiaan seemed genuinely surprised that the study of this bleak period in South African history could offer him any role models, people who shared his background and beliefs. In a country like South Africa the history of apartheid has to be approached sensitively, but that does not mean simplifying it into a morality play.

Titans such as Nelson Mandela can lose their power as role models if they become the only protagonists. Mandela's achievements are even greater when put into the context of other people's struggles and their attempts to undermine the apartheid state that imprisoned him. Beyers Naudé, though less significant than Nelson Mandela, proved to be an important focus for the enquiry since his actions interrupt the psyche of many students who believed that no one in such an elevated position would eschew the privileges of being a white Afrikaner during apartheid. Thato, a black African student at the same school, explained the significance for him of learning about apartheid through the life of Beyers Naudé:

> I really got touched by a man called Beyers Naudé ... he broke rank from his church. His church was basically an apartheid church, and for him a momentous event changed his point of view of South Africa, and he was the first person to take the step forward into South Africa's revolution ... To be honest he was basically fighting for Black people's rights and to me that's a lot. The whole apartheid church was founded by his father and if you're going to break rank and leave that church, he has a lot of integrity ... He's a man I truly respect for what he did for this country and that's one of the people that touched me personally.
>
> (Thato, Grade 9 student)

Thato's statement suggests that Naudé's actions could have changed his view of white people. No previous lessons had presented him with such figures, and his recognition of Naudé's sacrifice and integrity seems to have had a powerful impact on him and his understanding of the past.

The simplistic, Manichean approach to South African history is even more prevalent in London. The legacy of British people's opposition to apartheid in the 1970s and 1980s is to elevate famous figures such as Archbishop Desmond Tutu and Nelson Mandela, who had a number of streets named after him even while he was still in prison. This respect and veneration for a foreign freedom fighter becomes a cultural phenomenon and is passed down, forming part of the folk identity of the nation. The immense respect accorded to Mandela can lead to an equally strong vilification of anyone who might have been complicit in his suppression, which in Britain could be taken to mean all white South Africans. Olu, a student at a boys' school in Central London, explained how the Beyers Naudé enquiry altered his understanding of South African history:

> I look on it differently from I did before the enquiry, because I think I was closed minded about apartheid, how I thought every single white person was evil towards the Blacks, and even if it was a minority of them that tried to help the Black people and join forces with them to overthrow their own people, their own race

> ... they took a strain on their relationship with the whites just to help the Blacks have freedom, that changed my point of view.
>
> (Olu, London secondary school student)

Although the story of Beyers Naudé is not often recounted, Olu's comments suggest that an enquiry that focuses on a figure who challenges their preconceptions of South African history can benefit students' approach to history in general. It can show in quite stark terms that history is full of complexity, and that counter-stories form an important part of unravelling the complex stories.

Chapter 6

Black British history: Is there any Black in the Union Jack?

The significance of Black British history

In the autumn of 2014, we took part in two conferences in London on the theme of Black British history. One asked the question 'What's Happening in Black British History?', and the other had the rallying call 'Putting the Black in the Union Jack'. Both echoed the pugilism we have seen in every aspect of Black history we have explored, but the history of Black people in Britain seemed locked in a struggle for recognition, whereas the histories of Black people in Africa and the Americas had already won some respect and inclusion. Students in British schools and universities generally learn some Black history, but it is the history of slavery, African Empires, African American Civil Rights, apartheid. It is seldom the history of people of African descent and their contributions to Britain. There are few courses in British universities in which students can study Black British history. We have met one trainee history teacher in London who knows about key aspects of recent Black British history: he told us he had spent a year in a German university during his undergraduate degree, and had there taken a course on Black British history, taught by an Estonian.

Curriculum design and implementation involves choices: some possibilities are absent from the final plan. The significance of these absences has been highlighted by academics within the field of critical realism (Wilkinson, 2014). They show that some omissions damage the authenticity of the curriculum, and therefore the aims of education. Matthew Wilkinson (2014) explored the impact on Muslim students in secondary school of the absence of Muslim history from England's National Curriculum. His research confirms the importance of the 'identification stance' in the history curriculum (Barton and Levstik, 2004). Because the history of Muslims is missing from their curriculum, the Muslim boys he spoke to felt excluded from history. The same would be true for Black British students if Black British history is missing from the curriculum.

Furthermore, the absence of Black British history affects all young people. All need to learn how Britain has developed into the heterogeneous nation it is today. Black British history has also to be considered in relation to the majority master narrative. Michael Apple (2004) highlights the dangers of giving Black history 'the status of "add-ons" about the culture and history of "the Other"' (Apple, 2004: 178). Such an 'add-on' approach, which Apple calls *mentioning*, does not transform the history curriculum; it simply preserves the status of the master, white, narrative as the core of the curriculum.

There is a rich history of grassroots activism in the field of rights and relations within Britain's Black communities, akin to the history of the African American Civil Rights Movement, but it is not well known, despite the efforts of pioneers like Peter Fryer (1985). As a result, it is American Black history that is chosen by history departments for their schemes of work. There was a recommendation in 2008 that students in English secondary schools should be taught about 'modern British cultural and social history', but it was to be included in the citizenship curriculum, not the history framework (Maylor, 2010). This was never implemented, however, and the current National Curriculum for Citizenship (DfE, 2013) contains no references to history. It appears that the narrative of Black British history is seen primarily as a political field that cannot be safely admitted to the history curriculum. Including Black British history in the school curriculum entails a good deal more digging than was required for the topics we've covered so far. And the deliberate omission of Black British history to date demands much pugilism before teachers can attend to the choreography of lesson planning.

The 'safe' version of a multicultural curriculum is, in Michael Apple's words, 'one that does not interrupt the power of whiteness as "the human ordinary"' (Apple, 2004: 179). The power of whiteness and *Britishness* can remain undisturbed if the historical struggles against racial oppression that we teach are all struggles directed against racist Americans, Germans or South Africans and never Britons. The values of tolerance and individual liberty are endorsed when Black people are shown triumphing in history, just as white British people triumphed against the tyranny of Charles the First, or the evils of child labour in factories. However, Black triumphs are celebrated against American institutions, leaving students in English classrooms to declare, 'Martin Luther King Jr is important because he saved *us* from racism', a comment we have frequently heard as we observe classes.

So, why should Black British history be seen as significant enough to be included in mainstream history curricula? With respectful acknowledgement to our colleague Christine Counsell and her five 'R's (Counsell, 2004), we suggest three 'I's. We are indebted to our colleagues Alison Kitson and Jamie Byrom for working with us on the final formulation here. The first is *influence*: how someone, or something, produced consequences in their own time, or, how, long after their work was complete, someone continued to affect the way people functioned. The second is *insight*: how a person, place or event can show us what the key features of life were at a particular time and place in the past. Finally, as used throughout this book, *interruption of the psyche*: how someone or something challenges the conventional thinking about a situation in the past and dismantles assumptions made about history.

The well-known narrative of Black people in Britain begins with large numbers of Black and Asian settlers migrating to the 'mother country' from British colonies and then Commonwealth states after the Second World War. But diligent searching of archives and sources reveals the presence of Black people in Britain long before the arrival of the SS *Windrush* in 1948. Including early Black British settlers in the school history curriculum challenges the assumptions made about the homogeneity of past times.

In Tudor England the court bands of Henry VII and Henry VIII included a trumpeter of African descent named John Blanke (Fryer, 1985; Kaufmann, 2014). Why should John Blanke be considered significant? There were certainly many more white trumpeters at those courts, and there is no record of his having influenced the future of the King's music. Would his presence in a lesson about Tudor court life be anything other than a tokenistic gesture, an example of the *mentioning* that Michael Apple derides? If this was a discrete lesson inserted into the mainstream curriculum, perhaps for a special October initiative for Black History Month, the accusation could be legitimate. But John Blanke does have historical significance in terms of the third 'I', interrupting the psyche: since most people would assume that there were no Black people in Tudor England and that Black trumpeters arrived only in the twentieth century with jazz and a visit from Louis Armstrong, Blanke challenges preconceptions. John Blanke probably came to England through the dynastic political arrangements associated with the 1501 marriage of the Tudor prince Arthur to Catherine of Aragon, in whose kingdom Moors were part of fifteenth-century society. Blanke can be a source of evidence for that important dimension of understanding Tudor England as well as representing a small number of Black African people who we know made England proto-multicultural five hundred years ago (Onyeka, 2013). A further interruption to the psyche comes from the knowledge that these Black people were not in England because of slavery.

By the late eighteenth century people of African descent in Britain were significant in terms of their impact and influence in the campaigns to abolish the transatlantic slave trade and then the institution of slavery itself. Olaudah Equiano is now fairly well-known as a major campaigner, organizing and protesting with the Sons of Africa (Fryer, 1985; Walvin, 2000). Yet some schools still teach abolition principally through the life of William Wilberforce, who 'removed from England the guilt of the African slave trade', as it says on his monument in Westminster Abbey. Generally missing from coverage in schools of Britain's struggles in the two World Wars is the significant contribution made by Black and Asian soldiers and airmen from the colonies. Recently this contribution has been given media attention, notably in a book and TV series by David Olusoga (2014). These combatants' courageous contribution to the wars contrasts with the imperial response to their homelands after Britain's victory. The school curriculum should tell these stories from the perspectives of the Black and Asian people involved.

The history of the Black presence in Britain shows the complexity of change and continuity – a key historical concept – in our understanding of historical narratives. This chapter's enquiry considers the story of one significant Black activist, Claudia Jones, who strived throughout her life to bring about changes that could help the lives of her fellow Black citizens. Claudia's story is presented as one of hope in the face of myriad challenges, both personal and political. There are other Black British stories of achievement and success against heavy odds, such as those of Walter Tull, the first Black officer in the British Army in the First World War as well as the first Black professional outfield footballer in England, and Paul Stephenson, leader of the Bristol Bus Boycott in the 1960s and a prominent social and political activist since. However, there are also aspects of British history that show the continuity of racial tensions and discrimination that form the background to these achievements. It is these continuing challenges that form the focus of the historical perspective section in this chapter.

Historical perspective: the persistence of racism in Britain since Smethwick

Enoch Powell's speech on the issue of immigration in 1968 remains one of the most significant moments in the history of race relations in the UK since the docking of the SS *Windrush* in 1948. During his address to members of the Conservative Party, Powell highlighted the folly of any comparison between 'the American Negro and the Commonwealth Immigrant' (Powell, 1968). What many people found offensive in his speech was his casual dismissal of discrimination against immigrants in the UK as 'accidents' and 'personal misfortune'. Powell's speech tapped into latent fears of 'dark strangers' (Street, 2008). He delivered it two weeks after the assassination of Martin Luther King Jr and in the aftermath of urban unrest and riots in US cities. The titular warning, 'Rivers of Blood', is a direct reference to these riots. Powell's message was clear: immigration needed to be halted and reversed, and attempts at racial integration in Britain would lead to civil strife.

The views Powell expressed in that speech, like his reference to 'the Black man holding the whip-hand over the white man', found a large and supportive audience. The fear of the 'angry Black man' remains pervasive today and is a significant cause of discrimination in schools, the workplace and in wider civic life. Black people in Britain and the United States suffer disproportionately at the hands of the police; both have underachieved in relation to other groups in schools and so have remained economically less privileged (Sutherland, 2006). Perhaps it was these similarities that drew Malcolm X to the town of Smethwick in the West Midlands in 1965. Smethwick became notorious when its MP Peter Griffiths succeeded in a general election campaign rooted in attacking the Black immigrants in the area. Smethwick's local council planned to buy up properties on one of the town's more prominent streets in order to prevent more Black people settling there. In between high-profile international speaking events Malcolm X made the trip from London to Smethwick because he felt its immigrant population needed to assert itself against the hostile policies of the local authority. He observed that the plight of the Asian or West Indian immigrant was 'no different to that of the Southern Negro' (Street, 2008: 939). The sudden appearance of an American civil rights activist with a reputation for divisive and inflammatory rhetoric may well have motivated the MP from neighbouring Wolverhampton, Enoch Powell, to persist in his attempts to put immigration at the top of the national political agenda. Powell's success in doing so cost him his front-bench parliamentary career: he was sacked from the Shadow Cabinet by the leader of the Conservative Party the same year, 1968.

The activities of far-right organizations such as the National Front peaked in the decade after Powell's infamous speech. Objections to increased immigration and support for measures such as repatriation had a profound impact on immigrants and their children. By the mid-1970s two out of every five Black people in Britain were citizens by birth. The stories of those born in Britain give us powerful insights into the nature of race relations in Britain in the 1970s and 1980s, decades that were to be pivotal in the establishment of black communities – decades that have left scars (Hall, 1999). Areas of major cities with large Black populations were engulfed in disturbances by 1981 that many saw as a vindication of Powell's inflammatory racial rhetoric. The disturbances took the political establishment by surprise.

By the early 1970s the most stringent anti-immigration policies in Europe were in place in the UK. These policies pandered to the racist agenda of those who were inspired by Powell, although ministers continued to espouse the anti-discriminatory agenda introduced through successive Race Relations Acts. Consecutive governments turned a blind eye to the activities of fascist mobs that, between 1976 and 1981, were responsible for the murder of 31 Black and Asian people (Fryer, 1985). In 1978 Margaret Thatcher, as leader of the opposition, seemed to legitimate the growing hostility towards Black and Asian communities by suggesting, in a 1978 interview, that it was a natural response to a fear of 'being swamped by people of different cultures' (Margaret Thatcher Foundation, n.d.). Peter Fryer notes that 'culture' and 'colour' were being used as synonyms, and could only embolden right-wing thugs and the police who offered them protection and downplayed the racial motivation for their attacks.

Chris Mullard summed up the frustrations of Black Britons in his book *Black Britain* (1973). He wrote of the disaffection felt by the second generation at having their parents described as aliens because they were immigrants, and being seen themselves by most white people as interlopers who would never be British (Fryer, 1985). The situation came to a head in January 1981, when 13 Black people perished in a fire in Deptford, South London. As was becoming their custom, the Metropolitan Police quickly discounted any racist involvement in starting the fire, despite the area having been targeted by racists for years. In response to such overt police injustice a demonstration of 15,000 people, predominantly Black, marched the 10 miles from Deptford to Westminster to demand justice and security for their community. The response they got was an army of police tasked with 'reasserting authority', principally by searching and arresting every Black person they could. This operation was focused on the South London district of Brixton, which then became the first neighbourhood where Black people rebelled. These uprisings quickly spread around the country to almost every district with a sizeable ethnic minority population.

The decades that followed the uprisings of 1981 have been momentous ones in the history of race relations and for the future of Britain as a multicultural society. Stuart Hall (1999) wrote of the extent of changes to British society between the Scarman Report into the disturbances (1982) and the inquiry into the murder of Stephen Lawrence that culminated in the Macpherson report (1999). Recognition of the marginalization and alienation felt by Black people in England was the most progressive outcome of the Scarman inquiry. Although many saw this report as an inadequate response to the trouble that prompted it, Paul Gilroy (1992) argued that the Scarman Report was an important step towards challenging the prevalence of 'folk racism', meaning the racist stereotypes held by many to be straightforward common sense. Scarman explained that the social unrest in areas like Brixton was the result of a lack of economic opportunity and not, as many believed, the natural behaviour of a community that was inherently criminal. The behaviour of the police in deprived areas with high proportions of Black people fostered increased antagonism, and, according to Gilroy, actually helped generate a degree of solidarity amongst Black people. The increasing politicization of the Black community was also a reaction to high levels of support for the police and their actions amongst the wider public.

The victory of New Labour in 1997 seemed to usher in a new approach to race relations. The Conservative Party, which was believed by many to have held back progress in the 1980s, was now in opposition. Major public institutions were now under official scrutiny. Macpherson's identification of the Metropolitan Police Force as 'institutionally racist' in 1999 led to increased accountability and greater transparency. There was even a temporary drop in the number of Black men stopped and searched (Casciani, 2002). Hall (1999) counselled a cautious response to the apparent improvement in race relations. With issues now out in the open it became clear how long the road ahead was for those seeking a racially equitable society.

The front page of *The Independent* newspaper on 7 August 2015, however, reported that nearly every police force in England is still racist. Black people are still more likely to be stopped and searched by the police, and yet only a quarter of arrests lead to a conviction. Hall's warning could thus be described as prophetic. In 2011 an unarmed Black man, Mark Duggan, was shot dead in North London by police officers who released contradictory statements about their actions, suggesting the shooting might not have been lawful. The peaceful local demonstrations that immediately followed escalated into national rioting. As the scenes of anarchy played out on 24-hour news channels, English historian David Starkey discussed the cause of the riots on Newsnight. Starkey (2011) began his analysis with an admission that he turned to Powell's 1968 speech to help him understand the riots. The riots were clearly multiracial in nature, but according to Starkey they were proof that 'Black culture', which he equated with violent, anti-authoritarian nihilism, had been the principal cause. In Starkey's words 'the whites that took part had become Black' (Starkey, 2011). Starkey is not wholly representative of English society but his views, cloaked under the euphemism of 'plain speaking', suggest that the achievements in UK race relations since 1965 remain precarious.

Developing the Claudia Jones enquiry

In 1955 Claudia Jones was deported from the US, where she had spent most of her short life, because of her political views. She came to Britain. Jones had been born in Trinidad and lived there until she was nine years old. Since Trinidad was part of the British Empire until the early 1960s, and because she ended her life in Britain, we positioned Jones as a major figure in Black *British* history. Devoting a full six-lesson enquiry to the story of Claudia Jones, with historical significance the key conceptual focus, meant that we had to be clear about why she was significant. She is conspicuously absent from texts where one would expect to find her; there is no mention of her in *Staying Power* (Fryer, 1985), despite Fryer's detailed account of the Notting Hill Riot of 1958 and its aftermath. A recent scholarly work on Britain in the 1950s and 1960s by Sandbrook (2005) has a discussion about the origins of the Notting Hill Carnival, yet makes no mention of Claudia, who was one of its founders. There are only a few fragments of her autobiography, and only two major works have been written in recent decades that explore her life, one from the American perspective (Davies, 2008) and one from the British (Sherwood, 1999).

In terms of our three 'I's model, Jones had an *influence* on West Indian immigrants to Britain at the time, but the brief period for which she lived in England has meant that much of the pioneering work in tackling overt racism in Britain was seen to be done by others, such as members of the Campaign Against Race Discrimination (CARD), founded in January 1965 immediately after her death (Ramdin, 1999). In the same way, the few years in which London's carnival took place indoors (mainly in St Pancras Town Hall) under the guidance of Jones and a small team of colleagues have been totally overshadowed by the Notting Hill street festival that began after her death and which was led by Frank Critchlow, who came from the same part of Trinidad as Jones, and others.

Marika Sherwood, a founding member of the Black and Asian Studies Association, led the organization of a September 1996 symposium, including Jones's former colleagues and those who were influenced by her later to reflect on her life and work. Some 30 people responded, and

Sherwood's 1999 book was part of the result. But Jones does not appear to have been taken up as a major figure in the history of Black people in Britain in the way that Mary Seacole has (Operation Black Vote, 2013). Like Robert F. Williams in the USA (see Chapter 4), Jones presents an awkward story because of her unconventional activist stance – her communist ideology. Her courage and forthrightness in challenging convention, whether among the white establishment or her fellow Blacks, made Jones significant. British political activists were never quite sure how to position her, some considering her first and foremost as a communist, others principally as Black in her activism (Sherwood, 1999). Jones preferred not to be pigeonholed and absorbed herself in the work of challenging injustice and defending the oppressed. Claudia Jones interrupts the psyche by presenting us with a highly political and uncompromising Black woman who was rejected for her radical views; the intersectionality of her race and gender add to the interruption of the psyche, especially since she operated during a time when political life was still dominated by men.

The history of Black people in Britain inevitably involves migration stories, even now when so many Black British people were born in the UK. This gives their history a global dimension and draws in at least two different places in the world that might carry the term 'home'. The importance of place contributes to an understanding of Black British people's experiences. Claudia Jones's life took in travels from Trinidad to the US and finally to the UK in the mid-1950s. We first investigated her history for a Black History Month talk in 2011, and we matched her story with that of Somali people migrating to Britain (see Chapter 7) by following the common thread of nomadic life. The Somalis were historically nomadic, but Jones's itinerancy was brought about by economic circumstances and political activism. As we unravelled Jones's story, we discovered intriguing aspects that connected her to different places in London as well as those on the other side of the Atlantic. Her final resting place is in Highgate Cemetery, where her modest tombstone stands beside that of Karl Marx.

We knew of her connection to the origins of the Notting Hill Carnival, but then found that Jones's traditional commemorative blue plaque, which marks a place in London where an important historical person has resided, was actually on the streets of Notting Hill, not outside any of her residences (see Figure 6.1). This was to become the intriguing hook at the heart of the enquiry question: Why is Claudia Jones's blue plaque not outside her house and not in her homeland?

Figure 6.1: Claudia Jones's blue plaque in Notting Hill, London (authors' image)

There was one more place with a personal connection to Jones that drew us in to her story. Jones had contracted tuberculosis in the 1930s due to her family's poor living conditions during the Depression; when she came to London in the late 1950s, she was in and out of hospital with chest problems until her death in 1964 (Sherwood, 1999). The hospital to which she was regularly admitted in the early 1960s was St Stephen's in Fulham, where Robin Whitburn's mother had worked throughout the 1960s, and where he would often have to go after school or in the holidays – could Robin have passed Claudia as she was wheeled down a corridor to her ward? The hospital has gone, but the memory of place had made a connection. The annual Notting Hill carnival also makes a connection for those who might consider the significance of Claudia Jones, and the popularity and scale of the event could set up a 'felt difficulty' about the fate of its creator.

The blue plaque concept connected place with the idea of historical significance, which was to be at the centre of this enquiry. So we started the students off with an exercise that revolved around blue plaques. We had set them a preparatory homework task to research their local area, or an area of Central London they were familiar with, in order to find a blue plaque by physically visiting the place or seeing it online. This was to give them some familiarity with the notion of the blue plaque, so we could begin the first lesson with an 'odd-one-out' picture quiz. We chose four notable Caribbean men and women who have blue plaques in London: Mary Seacole, Marcus

Garvey, Claudia Jones and Bob Marley. We were surprised about Marley as we hadn't known of his stay in London, and the site is just around the corner from the Institute of Education where we had both studied and worked. Different aspects could have singled out any one of the four as 'odd'. Jones was the only one not from Jamaica; Mary Seacole was the only nineteenth-century figure; Garvey is the only one who is an official Jamaican National Hero. But the difference we were interested in would probably not be known to the students: Jones's plaque alone is not outside her residence. We hoped that the puzzle of finding out why this was would be the 'felt difficulty', and so it became the enquiry question.

The focus on place was then maintained through a brief exploration of Trinidad, and we again found some connections with famous Black figures: Frank Critchlow, Stokely Carmichael and Nicki Minaj were all born close to Claudia Jones's home in a district of Trinidad's capital, Port-of-Spain. The students are likely to have heard only of Minaj, but that familiar name gives them a point of access to the 'strange', and all four Trinidadians made their way as migrants to the United States (Minaj, Carmichael and Jones), or Britain (Critchlow). Both Minaj and Jones left Trinidad at a young age, and both went to New York, attending high schools there that focused on performing arts, although Jones could not afford a gown for her graduation.

Having sealed the aspects of 'familiar to strange', the enquiry then focused on analysing the factors that lead people to migrate as the Cumberbatches (Claudia's maiden name) had. The enquiry brings in a good deal of economic and social background on the countries to which Claudia belonged at different stages, including hardship in the West Indies after the First World War and the lure of the American Dream in the boom years of the 1920s. There is some discussion of the impact of the Great Depression in the US, along with details about how Jones's family suffered from her mother's death, her father's loss of income when he lost his job as a newspaper editor and became a janitor and Jones's contraction of tuberculosis by 1932.

In the second lesson of the enquiry we explained Jones's development as a political activist. This required some detailed explanation of the ideologies of capitalism and communism, rather than simply labeling Jones as a 'communist' and nearly all other Americans as 'capitalists'. We used a visual device recommended by one of Robin's student teachers, a pyramid representing the competitive hierarchy of capitalism and a pie-circle to represent the equal distribution of resources in a communist model. Taking time to explain these images helped the students to get a sense of why Jones found the idea of communism so appealing, especially at a time when the flaws in its implementation in the Soviet Union were not yet known. It was also important to introduce the intersectionality of race and class into the story of Jones's family, and to introduce the students to the story of the struggle of Black people in the north of the US, the brutal lynchings and the Ku Klux Klan. We also needed to explain the development of anti-communist feeling and eventual hysteria in the US, as Jones became a victim of the persecution of communists (and alleged communists) during the post-war period of McCarthyism. When commenting on her eventual expulsion from the US in 1955, Jones focused on the contradictions in American society:

> I was deported because I urged the prosecution of lynchers rather
> than prosecution of Communists and other democratic Americans
> who oppose the lynchers and big financiers and warmongers, the
> real advocates of force and violence in the USA.
>
> (Jones, quoted in Davies, 2008: 144)

We used this text as the basis for a discussion question comparing Jones's explanation for her expulsion with the official American government line, which the students had to infer.

Although the enquiry had begun as a study of a famous Black British figure of Caribbean heritage, it became clear that Jones's global identity had drawn in a great deal of American history as well. This is an important dynamic aspect of Black history and shows the complexity of diasporic identities. Half the enquiry was devoted to looking at Jones in Trinidad and the US to help us to understand her context and character before interpreting her significance in Britain. The enquiry called upon students to consider whether Jones should be commemorated in the US, before discussing her time in Britain; that was how the third lesson ended.

The investigation of Jones's years in England had to begin with the context of the West Indian migration that began with the arrival of the SS *Windrush* in 1948. We had material for this from a course that Robin had developed with Michelle Hussain (see Chapter 8) at St Mary's in Hendon, for a GCSE option briefly available from the AQA examination board on the history of multicultural Britain since 1945. The idea of migration to the imperial 'Mother Country' was introduced through the words of four men from the Caribbean who had arrived in Britain in the late 1940s. All expressed optimism about coming to the 'Mother Country':

> We've always looked forward to going to the mother country, and
> how we'd all be welcomed. We were taught that the people of this
> country would be welcoming, warm-hearted – that is what we
> were taught, it was driven into us, so it was a dream coming home.
>
> (Whitburn and Yemoh, 2012)

We then presented four video clips showing white English people expressing levels of concern about the 'coloured' immigrants, and provided explanations of the 'colour bar' and the discrimination concerning housing and jobs faced by West Indians throughout the 1950s and 1960s. When Claudia Jones came to England in 1955 she became immediately involved in campaigning for better conditions for her fellow Caribbean settlers.

The fifth lesson looks at Jones's activism, particularly in editing and publishing the *West Indian Gazette*, the first serious newspaper that dealt each month with the concerns of West Indians in Britain, the Caribbean, Africa and the US (Hinds, 2008). We discussed the significance of her newspaper in giving autonomy to the West Indian settlers as well as helping aspects of their assimilation in British society. In a video resource Donald Hinds describes Jones as a godmother to many West Indians in the UK, and the students discuss why he would give that interpretation of her. This penultimate lesson also looks at the race riots on the streets of north Kensington in 1958. These Notting Hill riots illustrated the racist violence that Black people were suffering from white youth gangs in London, Nottingham and elsewhere. The responses to the riots showed something of the ambivalence in English society toward the emerging issues of race relations. The judge handling the case of the white 'Teddy Boys' who were prosecuted for their part in the affray gave them quite tough sentences, hoping to show that Britain would not support racist violence. On the other hand, the government devoted more attention to worries about immigration and in 1962 passed the Commonwealth Immigrants Act, which restricted the numbers of non-white settlers that could be admitted to the UK. Jones responded by looking for ways of raising the spirits of her fellow West Indians, and this was how the first carnival events in London developed. Held to coincide with the period of carnival in the West Indies, the first London carnival was scheduled for February, and thus was staged indoors at St Pancras Town Hall.

The tragedy of Jones's death alone in her flat on Christmas Day 1964 marks a poignant end to the lesson, and reveals the constant pall of illness that marked her adult life. The final lesson of the enquiry is devoted to a debate about significance and a resolution of the enquiry question, ending with an assessment activity that makes use of the blue plaque on which it was based. The students choose where they would locate a commemorative plaque for Jones, producing an A4 poster showing their plaque, with a short argument for their choice of location.

Table 6.1 Outline of the seven-lesson enquiry on Claudia Jones

Why is Claudia Jones's blue plaque not outside her house and not in her homeland?

Lesson 1: How and why did Claudia Jones move from Trinidad to the United States?

Summary: Focus is on the concept of significance as well as Claudia's early life. Students prepare for the lesson by exploring local blue plaques or other forms of remembrance and why the people have been remembered. This sets up the enquiry question and the felt difficulty: What makes Claudia Jones special? The lesson then looks at her early life in Trinidad, linking her to other famous migrants from Port-of-Spain and the search for self-improvement overseas. The lure of the American Dream and the problems that faced the Joneses instead, first because of racism and then the Depression of the 1930s, are the focus of the last part of the lesson.

Activities include: Using students' preparation on blue plaques to help tackle the 'odd-one-out' exercise on Bob Marley, Mary Seacole, Marcus Garvey and Claudia Jones. The initial explanation of her childhood shows Claudia being born close to others who went on to migrate from Trinidad: Stokely Carmichael, Frank Critchlow and Nicki Minaj. Consider the questions: *Why would Claudia's family decide to move from Trinidad to the United States? Why might this seem a surprising decision for a black Caribbean family to make?* Use images showing the idea of the American Dream, and students' own knowledge of racism in the US, to speculate on challenges. The Depression and its impact are examined as a plenary.

Lesson 2: How and why did Claudia Jones become a political activist in the US?

Summary: The key theme is considering political activism and how it developed among some Americans during the years of the Depression, beginning with an examination of the notion of a 'radical activist'. The ideologies of capitalism and communism are explored, and students consider how poor people might have responded ideologically to the changing circumstances in the US during the 1920s and 1930s.

Activities include: The potential impact of the Depression, and the specific circumstances for the Joneses, are examined using two levels of questioning for self-selected differentiation: Standard: *How and why might Claudia Jones change her mind about the new life her family had started in the US?* Super: *Why might Claudia Jones be ready to challenge the way the American system operated in the 1930s?* Students then explore the meanings of 'radical' and 'activist'. Capitalism and communism are presented with two simple diagrams: a triangle, to show the drive to the top of the capitalist competition, and a circle divided into equal sectors to show the ideal of communist equality.

Lessons 3: Should Claudia Jones have a commemorative plaque in the USA?

Summary: American fears of communism, both before and after the Second World War, are the background to understanding the McCarthy era and Jones's persecution and eventual deportation from the US in 1955. The threat Jones posed to the American establishment is explored through her own words: 'I was deported because I urged the prosecution of lynchers rather than prosecution of Communists.' The students then consider how significant Jones might be for American history. Her remarkable, yet futile, confrontation of the establishment, as a radical Black woman, might lead students to question the traditional male-dominated picture of African-American resistance, either in judicial or militant activism.

Activities include: After establishing the pattern of America's hostility towards communism, students compare Claudia's explanation of her prosecution with the government view. There is then a debate on whether she should have a commemorative plaque in the USA, and how significant Claudia Jones is for American history.

Lesson 4: What were the challenges facing West Indian migrants in Britain in the 1950s?

Summary: The experiences of West Indian migrants to the UK in the 1950s are explored to show the challenges of assimilation and autonomy in their lives. Students examine the naïveté of some of their initial hopes and their vision of Britain as 'the mother country', and consider how that idealism was challenged by their growing experiences of racism in the 1950s. Claudia's arrival in the UK in 1955 came at a time when routine daily discrimination had been established. A 'colour bar' affected housing, employment and leisure.

Activities include: Short video clips of West Indians who arrived in the early 1950s and expressed confidence in the 'mother country' lead to a discussion about their possible naïveté. The 'colour bar' and 'Black tax' are again explained through video clips, and the students discuss why it would be so hard for West Indians to try to assimilate into Britain at the time. Link this to Jones through the key question: *Why would Claudia Jones be especially concerned with the welfare of West Indian migrants in Britain?*

Lesson 5: How far did the campaigns of Claudia Jones help to tackle the problems of racism in Britain?

Summary: Jones's activism is clear in the *West Indian Gazette*, which she set up soon after her arrival in Britain in 1955. She was involved in a range of spheres, including campaigns against apartheid and the atom bomb. Her exceptional drive is clear from interviews with colleagues, and the cost to her health is also explained. Jones was a pioneer at a time of great challenge. The *Gazette* was the first newspaper for the Caribbean community in Britain.

Activities include: Considering how Jones attempted to use her journalistic experience to help the West Indians through a monthly newspaper, and how such a publication could be part of both assimilation and autonomy. Students then examine a letter that was sent by a UK Ku Klux Klan member to Jones, and consider how well she would have been prepared to cope with it. A video clip of Bill Strachan and Trevor Carter discussing Jones establishes some of the gender issues in the British movement to help Black immigrants, and also shows the drive and ambition that Jones brought to campaigning. The scope of her activism is shown in video clips about her involvement in the early anti-apartheid movement in Britain, as well as anti-nuclear weapons campaigns and global feminism.

Lesson 6: How did events in Notting Hill in 1958 confront West Indians in Britain and how did Claudia Jones help them respond?

Summary: The stark experience of racism at the time was illustrated in the riots in Notting Hill, West London, in 1958, when issues of mixed relationships and raw prejudice led to violence against Black Britons from young white 'Teddy Boys'. The range of responses in London shows the ambiguities in British race relations, with the judiciary condemning racist violence, but the government rushing to curb further immigration. The strong connection is shown between Jones's indoor carnivals in London each February and Caribbean Carnival, before the former was switched to August and to the streets of Notting Hill after Claudia's death.

Activities include: Viewing a documentary section showing the background to the riots, with Alfred Harvey helping to explain the build-up of tension in the area of Notting Hill, both in the immediate weeks of the summer of 1958 and in the years preceding it. Students can consider short-term causes and long-term influences here. The responses of key groups are considered: judges, the government, Caribbean migrants and some racist British people, including Oswald Mosley, and students examine how Jones responded.

Lesson 7: Where should Claudia Jones's commemorative plaque be placed?

Summary and activities: Claudia Jones's significance is the subject of a class debate and the final assessment exercise, in which students decide where her commemorative plaque should be placed – in Trinidad, the USA or London – and present their design and explanation. There are videos and written texts that indicate Claudia's significance.

Abdul Mohamud and Robin Whitburn

Transforming the learning and teaching of Black British history

The terrorist attacks in London in July 2005 stirred up anxieties about national identity and young people's sense of 'Britishness'. That young British citizens could become so disaffected that they perpetrated such atrocities caused alarm. In 2006 future prime minister, Gordon Brown, then still Chancellor of the Exchequer, proposed that Britain's history curriculum could counter the decline of British morale and contribute to the development of a positive British identity:

> And we should not recoil from our national history – rather we should make it more central to our education. I propose that British history should be given much more prominence in the curriculum, not just dates, places and names, nor just a set of unconnected facts, but a narrative that encompasses our history.
>
> (Brown, 2006)

Such anxieties persist and the inculcation of 'British values' is now expected of all maintained schools and qualified teachers in England (DfE, 2014). Brown called for a singular narrative in a manner not dissimilar to that of Michael Gove, the Education Secretary of the Conservative–Liberal Democrat Coalition Government that followed his (Gove, 2011).

The challenges mounted by Enoch Powell and others against greater racial diversity in British society show that the presence of Black communities in Britain has often been seen as a threat to British identity. Studying the history of Black communities would be seen by many people as counterproductive to the development of national unity. However, as Osler (2009) argues, diversity doesn't inevitably imply a lack of solidarity or a threat to national identity. We have researched the impact of teaching enquiries about Black British history in the 1950s and 1960s, including the one on Claudia Jones. Interestingly, for many students, their respect for 'Britishness' increased thanks to their critical engagement with the challenging themes and issues presented in the analysis of post-war race relations. Rather than being divisive, engaging with the murky and controversial past and working through tough questions gave students an appreciation of the complexity of the past. Ajit, an Asian student at Bishop's High School, a multicultural and co-educational Church of England comprehensive in North London, commented:

When you learn about the country that you are living in, you feel more assured that your country can move forward from problems.

(Ajit, Bishop's High School student)

Having explored the contradictions and injustices in Britain's history, the students gained greater respect for the universally desirable values of 'tolerance, freedom and fairness' that Britishness is seen to promote (DfE, 2014). As Carl, a white British student at Bishop's, affirms, students appreciated the power of change in British society:

We learnt about the Notting Hill riots, and how it was basically police against Black citizens, and how crazy it was before; the only way to be heard was by rioting. Whereas you see today at the carnival it's integrated. There are Black and white police, and people of difference races enjoying it. *You can see how far we have come as a nation.*

(Carl, Bishop's High School student; emphasis added)

Studying the struggles of Black and Asian people in post-imperial Britain is not antithetical to building a confident sense of Britishness. This would be the case in any school, whether or not its population was ethnically diverse. Ellen, a white student at Bishop's, of New Zealand heritage, spoke for a number of students:

I think it's good to learn the trials that people go through to get where we are today. It's good to learn and respect that ... I think it would still matter in an all-white school. People need to know and respect the history that is still there.

(Ellen, Bishop's High School student)

The students reflected on the emphasis in English schools on teaching and learning about American race relations, and the approach taken at Bishop's School of focusing on Black British history as well as the Civil Rights Movement. Though they appreciated and enjoyed the American history, they questioned the rationale for British students learning it and not the history of British race relations. Jeron, a student of Black British Caribbean heritage, remarked:

No one really knew we had a break up in this country. People think that the civil rights struggle or human rights struggle was only in America, so they got credit for everything. And me being Caribbean, it was like my people struggled as well.

(Jeron, Bishop's High School student)

Jeron's comment highlights the importance of presenting the struggles for racial justice that we have taught. Jeron wanted to see 'his people' (Black British Caribbeans) feature in the history studied at his school; for him the 'credit' for struggle and achievement was very important.

In the development of a history curriculum in Britain's multicultural society, positive agents of change – rather than victims – are essential to ensure that Black students are not left feeling discouraged as a result of engaging only with negative histories. Some of the Black boys who were part of a research group at Broadwood School, a boys' comprehensive in Central London, also affirmed the importance of identifying with Black British figures in history when they discussed the enquiries they had pursued in Year 7, which included the Claudia Jones enquiry.

Interviewer: Which topic of the ones you've studied was most significant to you personally and why?

Marvin: I think it was the Claudia Jones one because part of it was about the Jamaicans and Caribbeans coming over to England and that's what my nan did as well, and I liked studying that.

Sean: The topic that was most significant for me was when we learnt about Claudia Jones as well because I've been to Notting Hill carnival a few times and it's actually quite exciting ... I wondered a few times who created it, and why it was created interested me.

Carson: I liked the Claudia Jones one because she was fighting for Black people's rights, because at the time they were disrespected and weren't treated as equals to white people ... and even though she was put into prison, she was still fighting for Black people's rights, which means she was a strong-willed person.

(Interview with Year 7 students at Broadwood School)

It is important that all students in English schools have the opportunity to study the struggles and triumphs of Black people in Britain in the development of our diverse society, and it is vital that young people from the groups who had to bear the burdens of these struggles see that their history lessons do justice to their heritage.

Chapter 7

British Somali history: Innovation in Black British history

Bringing British Somali history to schools

The popular assumption is that Somalis began to arrive in the UK only recently, from a ravaged country with too few resources to nourish its own people let alone contribute to the world's welfare. Media accounts of Somalia dwell on the perils of famine and civil war, and on sensational dramas of piracy on the Indian Ocean. All this suggests the new arrivals cannot play a constructive part in the development of multicultural Britain (Gardham, 2015). The conventional history of Black people in the UK has generally been limited to the post-1945 narrative of the 'Windrush generations', as if recent arrivals are somehow less worthy of acceptance and incorporation into a Black British story. The demonization of Somalis by the media, combined with growing Islamophobia, has produced a narrative of Somalis as unworthy of equality with other Black British people, and even potentially dangerous to Britain (Harris, 2004).

The antagonisms generated by these manipulated histories and myths were highlighted in a television programme presented by the prominent, controversial, Black British commentator Darcus Howe. Entitled *Who you Callin' a Nigger?* (2004) the programme gave a bleak portrayal of multicultural diversity in Britain's urban centres. Howe devoted a major part of his exposé to street violence between 'West Indians and Somalis' in South East London:

> I journeyed through Woolwich and Plumstead, where thousands of Somali refugees are settling. The Caribbean community is mostly unwelcoming. Some visit on Somalis the same kind of racial abuse we suffered in the period of early migration. Dissenters to this reactionary view are few and far between. 'They are taking our houses. They are getting social benefits which are denied to us. Their children are overcrowding our schools'.

> (Howe, 2004)

117

Howe was not fabricating these tensions. We have both witnessed these divisions in our classrooms, and Abdul experienced such hostility first-hand growing up in Central London. The programme failed to present positive stories of Somali communities in Britain. Mainstream media suggest that nothing good could come from Somalia or its dispersed people around the world. For the 30,000 Somali pupils studying in London's secondary schools this bleak perception can create difficulties (Kahin, 1997; Rasmussen, 2011).

If the media do not present a balanced view, one hopes that schools would make the effort to put matters straight. Sadly, the negative preconceptions of the media and society seem to extend to school history departments. We were stunned to hear that a teacher who wanted to develop our British Somali history enquiry in her school was ridiculed by her head of department, who scoffed at the notion of teaching six lessons about 'pirates'. Without the support of their teachers, it is the students who have to carry the burden of creating a historical interpretation that is accurate and just. British Somali students in our schools face a double injustice: first, to be unfairly portrayed and, second, to have to disprove the negative portrayals of your community with no help from your teachers. Yet inclusive history can address the damage done through stereotypes and prejudice, and help to build a greater sense of confidence among students and possibly greater cohesion. For Abdul, discovering this history of his people enabled him to take pride in aspects of British history. But without his own people's inclusion in British history, he struggled to find personal and communal pride in the nation's story, although he knew the narratives well.

In developing better history education in schools, history teachers and scholars challenge the misconceptions students have in relation to key metacognitive historical concepts such as causation and change (Lee and Shemilt, 2004; Conway, 2006). Less attention is paid to misconceptions that impede students' grasp of substantive content, although this is essential for the development of strong, culturally responsive pedagogy and curricula (Ladson-Billings, 1995). Teachers who want to guide their students through enquiries that explore hidden histories must attend to the rigour of its pedagogical processes, but also defend the relevance of a potentially maligned and misrepresented community. The negative stereotypes of Somalis in Britain were the 'familiar' that Wineburg identifies in historical thinking (2001), that is the prelude, whereas exploration of the 'strange' takes in the history of Somali people in Britain since 1870.

We consistently thought of the people at the heart of this enquiry as British Somalis in contemporary society, and were interested in the way they became British. However, it was difficult to lead teachers in that direction:

they constantly referred to the work as 'Somali history', not British Somali history. Even though we were clear about the inclusive 'pugilism' involved, others wanted to position the history – and us – very narrowly. We were told that the work 'sounds interesting' but wouldn't be relevant to that school because 'there aren't many Somalis here'. Paradoxically, we also met resistance from a school where there *were* Somali students because the senior leaders thought it would be too partisan to focus on just *their* history for six lessons. We were adamant that we wanted to see the enquiry as part of any school's approach to *British* history, but the interpretation of 'British' in schools can be narrow (Maylor, 2010).

Perhaps it was too challenging for teachers to accept the interruption of their psyche about the Horn of Africa. Nurtured on a diet of Comic Relief and Oxfam posters through the late twentieth century, they might accept a humanitarian approach to considering Ethiopian or Somali narratives, but balk at finding out more about people they consider to have only a marginal connection to Britain. The lack of enthusiasm and engagement with the idea of British Somali history could also reflect some weariness with multiculturalism. With a number of prominent politicians and commentators speaking out against the idea (see Cremin and Warwick, 2008), it can be fashionable to adopt a sceptical tone to multicultural curricula, and some history teachers might resist doing any more than they think they have to, usually teaching only the slave trade and civil rights.

Those teachers who do consider the historical narrative emerging from this enquiry find an abundance of connections to contemporary concerns about identity and national values (Osler, 2009). The particular concerns in recent years about the allegiance of Muslims in Britain, particularly after the terrorist attacks of July 2005, should spur schools to consider the longevity of the migration of Somali Muslims to Britain throughout the twentieth century and the honour of the Somali men who fought bravely to defend Britain in both world wars (Jordan, 2004). Although there were only a few hundred Somali men in Britain before 1950, their significance lies, like John Blanke's in Tudor England, in the way their presence and involvement in Britain disturbs our contemporary views about the abnormality of certain ethnic groups' presence in our midst.

The longstanding presence of mosques in certain British port communities, where Somalis and other Muslim seamen lived, suggests that Islam has not always been seen as a hostile force in the UK. Troubles in Somalia itself undoubtedly increased the settlement of Somali people in urban British centres since 1990, but we present research that shows a diverse pattern of Somali migration to the UK for over one hundred years and reveals complex interaction between the Muslim nomads from the Horn of Africa and British people. This history suggests that we should not propose a dichotomy between assimilation and autonomy in migrant communities, but look for their complementary interaction in the lives of minority peoples who are decidedly British. Other Black British communities already had significant narratives that confirmed their value to the nation, such as the Caribbean contribution to public services after 1948, and this has helped develop their sense of identity as Black and British. The Somalis had no such narratives when settling in this foreign land. We hoped that developing this enquiry for schools would contribute to the wider dissemination of a significant narrative of British Somali history.

Historical perspective: British Somali history

When we began working on the history of Somali peoples in Britain in 2011 the popular image of Somalia was poor, following twenty years of political anarchy. Stories of the country being used as a base for Islamic terrorists and as the home for the highest-profile pirates of modern times reverberated around the world on 24-hour news channels and the internet. Underlining the image of the archetypal failed state, the United Nations declared the return of famine to the country in July 2011, with an estimated 250,000 perishing as a result (Seal and Bailey, 2013). The capital, Mogadishu, had become a synonym for chaos and depravity, and was the title of a dark play set in a London school after the riots of August 2011 (Harper, 2012). A BBC reporter horrified by the riots described their epicentre, Tottenham, as 'looking like Mogadishu' (Harper, 2012).

Since the collapse of the country's central authority in 1990, it seems that nothing but despair has come out of Somalia. It is difficult to present an alternative to the narrative that focuses on the consequences of political breakdown. The images on television of adolescents wielding machine guns, skeletal women clutching emaciated children and villainous pirates are real enough. What is not reported are the causes of such suffering and anarchy. This has coloured people's view of Somalia.

The huge success of Hollywood films such as *Black Hawk Down* and *Captain Phillips* reflect the public's appetite for representations of the dystopian consequences of Somalia's political turmoil. The reason why a once flourishing fishing coast has become home to criminal extortionists is seldom explored and there is a dearth of academic publications on Somali political history. In the absence of positive narratives, negative storylines are perpetuated: the victims are the Somali diaspora, which has spread all over the world since 1990. Many of the diaspora's members are too young to recall a national narrative that didn't have at its core tribal conflict and sustained lawlessness. Older Somali migrants hope for an improvement in the political situation and many view their residency in their adopted country as temporary. Most of the 100,000 Somalis in Britain who were born in Somalia live in Liverpool, Bristol, Cardiff and London. Others have more recently settled in Leicester and Birmingham, but their significant presence in port cities gives some hints about the long-standing Somali presence in Britain. This population in fact predates the current turmoil, and we can find glimpses of their role in Britain's economic and social history as far back as 1870.

The opening of the Suez Canal in November 1869 was a major milestone in Britain's growth as an imperial power, greatly reducing the time it took to travel to and from Britain's most important colony, India. The Red Sea and the Indian Ocean became among the busiest shipping lanes in the world and, in an era of colonial rivalry, the British were anxious to safeguard the huge amount of commercial shipping that passed through. This entailed the acquisition of territory either side of this sea route that might have been used by Britain's opponents to endanger the profitable trade with India and the Far East. The territory that would later become the Somali Republic was slowly acquired by Britain through a series of treaties with regional and colonial powers. But Anglo–Egyptian suzerainty over northern Somalia collapsed with the rise of the self-proclaimed Mahdi, an influential Muslim cleric, in Sudan in the 1880s. In order to protect supply routes to Britain's main Indian Ocean port, Aden, officials in Whitehall ordered the establishment of a British Protectorate in Somaliland in 1888.

Although the destiny of the protectorate was of secondary importance to the British, the Italians had great ambitions for their possessions in Somalia, especially after they were humiliatingly defeated by Ethiopia on the plains of Adowa in 1896. One reason for Britain's reluctant occupation of Somaliland was the recent memory of the wars against the Mahdi in the Sudan. The Mahdi's 'Mad Mullah' moniker given by the British press would later be transferred to Somali leader Sayyid Mohammed Abdille Hassan, as he and his devout army of Dervishes fought against the host of nations that had expanded their control over the Somali 'nation' by 1900. Hassan's revolt lasted for 20 years, until 1920, when the RAF, under the direction of Secretary of State for War Winston Churchill, made pioneering use of aerial bombardment and destroyed Hassan's land forces. Hassan died shortly afterwards of influenza and would later be remembered as a national hero.

Not all Somalis resisted foreign influence. The clans around the coast prospered from the growth in demand for meat and other goods, and the young men witnessed the daily passage of merchant and military vessels. The promise of distant travel and adventure lured them into employment on the ships. One of the few detailed accounts we have of Somali communities in early-twentieth-century Britain comes from the biography of a Somali seaman, Ibrahim Ismaa'il. His story is remarkable on a number of levels, not least for the circumstances in which it was written. Eugene Gaspard-Marin, a Belgian anarchist and intrepid traveller, met Ibrahim Ismaa'il at a mosque in Cardiff's Tiger Bay. After the two struck up an unlikely friendship Ismaa'il agreed to travel with Gaspard around England.

In Gaspard's record of Ismaa'il's story, the two visited London and were denied lodgings in a number of hostels and hotels. Although both were foreign nomads with a love for storytelling and poetry, only Gaspard was offered a room by the manager of the Rowntree boarding house in King's Cross. Such discrimination was not new to Ismaa'il, who had witnessed the anti-immigrant riots that engulfed Cardiff in 1919 when white British servicemen returning from the trenches of the Western Front directed their frustrations over the lack of employment at the Black and Asian residents of Tiger Bay. Even when Ismaa'il arrived at an anarchist commune in the Cotswolds as Gaspard's guest he slept with a revolver under his pillow for fear of being attacked by his white hosts, a fear he later realized was unfounded as his hosts received him fully into their community. It was here that Ismaa'il recounted his experiences at length to Gaspard, and one story in particular offers valuable insights into the relationship between migrants of different backgrounds in early-twentieth-century Britain.

The following is the full account of Ismaa'il's interaction aboard a British Merchant vessel with a West Indian man referred to only as 'Moses'.

The Story of Ismaa'il and Moses

I joined a ship which went to Liverpool, then to Lisbon. I was the only Somali on board; the rest of the crew consisted of a West Indian called Moses, a German, a Pole, and two jolly Irishmen. The German and I became great friends.

Moses and I were put on the same watch: Moses worked the port boiler, and I the starboard boiler. The shovel belonging to my boiler was a new one but the other one was old and had an impaired edge which made it more difficult to work; invariably

Moses would grab the new shovel which had been left on my side, and I had to use the bad one.

After a good many days I told him: 'It is not fair that you should use the good shovel all of the time'. He gave no answer. At our next watch I made sure to grab hold of it before him. He tried to snatch it from me, but I refused to let go. Then he poured upon me a torrent of insults which meant very little to me as I could hardly understand them. After we had cleaned our fires, Moses took his slice and sliced his three fires, I did the same – for by working in unison it is possible to get up steam much quicker. Having finished, I put my slice on my ash-pit damper, and leaned on my shovel, while Moses was finishing his last fire, the nearest to me. When he finally pulled out the red hot slice from the furnace, he hurled it at me with both hands saying 'Take it you Arab bastard'. I pulled myself up and just escaped the tool, which did no more than graze my thighs.

For the moment I remained dumbfounded. Then I thought to myself; Moses has tried to kill you, and has missed; now your turn, and don't miss him! I did not utter a sound. The Pole and the German who had kept the previous watch were still waiting for us to pass the ashes on to them. One shouted 'hurry up, we want to go to bed'. I said to Moses with composure: 'Let us give them the ashes'. 'All right' he answered. I took the shovel while he was holding the sack open. I put in a few shovelfuls and then I took up the hammer which I had placed handle upwards by my side and I aimed at his skull. Fortunately for him – and still more fortunately for me – he raised his head at that very moment and the hammer missed him! It was his turn to be paralysed with stupor. Then we rushed at each other and fought like two wild animals until we were exhausted.

Then Moses tried to argue he had no intention to kill me, but he failed to convince me. I urged him to try to recognize the truth: we have both tried to murder one another, but we have shown ourselves very bad marksmen. At the same time we realised what fools we had been. If one of us had killed the other he would have been hanged and nobody would have cared about either of us. And after that we became good friends.

(Ismaa'il, quoted in Pankhurst, 1977: 375–6)

The story of Ismaa'il and Moses is one of hope. It illustrates how people can overcome ethnic and cultural divisions and respect one another through the things that unite them. The life Ismaa'il describes aboard the boat affirms the benefits of multiculturalism. The story reminds us that good history education is not about extolling the virtues of good men and using the lives of villainous figures as cautionary tales. Ismaa'il's experiences on board that ship reflect the diversity of experience of the British Somali community whilst also endorsing the longevity of their presence and their small but important role in Britain's national story.

Developing the British Somali history enquiry

This history was a key part of our first work together in the autumn of 2011. Robin Whitburn had been asked to deliver a series of talks to council employees in the London boroughs of Merton and Sutton during Black History Month. As the talks were to be about Black British history, he invited Abdul Mohamud to join him, and suggested he might like to focus one talk on the history of the Somali communities as he is of Somali heritage. This set us to unearthing histories neither of us had known or envisaged. Virtually nothing had been written about the history of Somalis in Britain, and little in English on the history of Somalia, so Abdul had to rely on his own cultural knowledge and internet resources. The most important thing that came out of that first exposition on Somalis in Britain was the telling metaphor of the packed and unpacked suitcase, which we used to engage people with changes in the way Somali people interacted with Britain. The packed suitcase represented the Somalis' nomadic lifestyle in Africa, and we contrasted it with its eventual unpacking, to convey the idea of a settled existence in Britain.

This metaphor was to play a central role in the classroom enquiry, and fashioned the enquiry question itself: Why did the Somalis finally decide to unpack their suitcases in Britain? We wanted the metaphor to connect with two vital substantive concepts that would help students explore the lives of immigrants in Britain: assimilation and autonomy. These resonated with our image of unpacked and packed suitcases. When we first taught the enquiry, we brought an old-fashioned suitcase into the classroom. The students found it easier to tackle the metaphor and its conceptual references when they had a tangible object to represent it. In the first two schools where we taught the enquiry, Abdul and I presented the students with a dramatic role-play: a Somali at Paddington Station in 1950, on the way to Cardiff, was interviewed for radio about his intentions in coming to Britain. The suitcase was a key part of the drama. When a metaphor played such an important part in developing students' conceptual understanding in a topic, it was clearly important to spend time enabling them to grasp its meanings.

The next stage of the enquiry was to find sources that could engage the students with these concepts of autonomy and assimilation and lead them to the notion of the suitcase. Rarely do we tell students the key ideas in a lesson: we want them to be able to work them out through discussion and interrogation of sources. We found two photographs from Paul Gilroy's photographic history of Black Britain (2007), and these enabled us to give the students some idea of the complexity of the lives of Somali men who came to Britain well before the migrations at the end of the twentieth century. The pictures showed Somali men in Cardiff in 1950 in two very distinct milieux: one showed them at prayer in the Peel Street mosque wearing *kofi* and *ma'awiis*, the traditional hat and sarong of Somali men, and the second showed them in the living room of a boarding house in suits and ties. The photographs were taken by Bert Handy, who in the years immediately after the Second World War captured scenes in Butetown, Cardiff, where diverse racial groups had been living as neighbours for decades.

Gilroy gave no explanation of the background to these two pictures; the caption for that of the mosque was simply '1950'. This invited us to extend our historical knowledge and imagination to recognize the presence in Cardiff of Muslim men, including Somalis, for far longer than is generally assumed. With no information about the provenance of the pictures, the students could speculate freely about the world of these men and consider how the concepts of assimilation and autonomy might be playing out in their lives. We set them on the same journey that we had followed, and simply put the photo on the screen in the classroom, along with the caption ('1950'), and the key questions: Where are these men? Who are they? We hoped this would interrupt the psyche by eliciting their assumptions about the likely location of Muslims at prayer in the middle of the twentieth century, and then it would be revealed that this mosque was in Wales.

The two Cardiff photographs were used for a single lesson taught in East London. When we contemplated building a whole six-lesson enquiry on British Somali history, we realized that we would need more substantial resources to engage the students and flesh out the lives of the men we had discovered. This prompted us to visit Cardiff and the Butetown History and Arts Centre, where Glenn Jordan introduced us to his work on Somali elders (Jordan, 2004). These inspiring characters embodied the complexities we were exploring regarding Somali people's encounters with Britain. Jordan's project had photographed the leading men in Cardiff's Somali communities and recorded something of their personal histories. Most of them had been seamen, and several fought for Britain in the Merchant Navy in the Second World War and other conflicts. Some had families in Somalia, but some had married and raised mixed-race families with British women. Their portraits and stories evinced pride in their Somali identities, but they also appeared at ease in British society. One man captured our attention immediately, and we made him a cornerstone of the enquiry. His name was Mohamoud Kalinle, and his picture was compelling (see Figure 7.1).

Figure 7.1: Mohamoud Kalinle (image reproduced by kind permission of Glenn Jordan/Butetown Heritage and Arts Centre)

Kalinle was dressed in well-worn Western clothes, apart from his kofi, and he was looking down, avoiding the gaze of the camera. Attached somewhat haphazardly across his overcoat were five medals from his service in the British armed forces. He was clearly proud of his contribution to the defence of his adopted country, as there was no compulsion for him to wear the medals in public, but he wasn't conforming to the usual way of wearing them. Was there an ambivalence in his patriotism, perhaps? We warmed to his non-conformity, and his oral testimony sparked even greater interest:

> I was born in Arabsiyo in 1912. Arabsiyo is a small town west of Hargeisa and is known for its many farms. My father owned many horses. I was born near a famous tree called Agamso in Arabsiyo. We used to live in a Somali traditional tent. I moved to Djibouti when I was twelve years old to join my uncle. I owned a small boat to ferry people off the big ships in Djibouti and I was making a lot of money for the time. We used to have a lot of camels but we didn't spend much time with them. There is no Somali without camels. Eventually I sold my boat and went to Marseilles, France, to look for jobs. I left Marseilles and went to Paris and from there to Le Havre and eventually I came to Dover. From there I came to Cardiff in 1937 and have lived here ever since.
>
> I joined the Merchant Navy and later the Royal Navy and worked as a fireman and donkeyman in the engine room. I worked on ships and destroyers. I fought in the Second World War, helping to destroy some ships and two fighter aircraft in Malta. I was the leader of the Somali Community in Cardiff and also one of the Trustees of the Mosque on Maria Street. My wife was from Wales. Her name was Doreen and her Somali name was Halima. She died in June 2004. We have a son called Jama, who is fifty-nine years old.
>
> (Kalinle, quoted in Jordan, 2004: 182–3)

That one's birthplace would be marked by a tree spoke volumes about nomadic life in Somalia, and Kalinle's itinerant seafaring echoed that. Whilst these aspects made Kalinle strongly traditional, his marriage to Doreen, presumably shortly after the Second World War, showed his integration into British life. Nonetheless, it seemed that the assimilation was not one-sided, as Doreen took a Somali name. We felt that Kalinle was a brilliant source for students to examine for aspects of autonomy and assimilation. When we came to consider an engaging assessment activity for the enquiry, we decided to get the students to write a book proposal that Kalinle would submit for his autobiography, with its book cover, chapter synopses and recommendations from prominent citizens, like the Mayor of Cardiff and Mo Farah.

We now had sufficient material to form an enquiry that revealed a story of Somali people in Britain, contributing not only to the industrializing economy of the predominant global economic power of the Victorian age, but also to the defence of the nation in wars for over a century. The lessons outlined the history of the British Empire in the mid-nineteenth century, along with the development of the Suez Canal that brought British trade and shipping into contact with the Somali coast and peoples for the first time. This took us to the first Somali sailors in Cardiff in 1870, and to the contribution of Somali sailors to both World Wars. We found an intriguing story of the Cardiff race riot of 1919 in Fryer's 1985 book *Staying Power*, which reproduced it from an earlier journal article by Richard Pankhurst (1977). The account came from autobiographical fragments collected by Pankhurst from the Whiteway colony in the Cotswolds, where a Somali man called Ibrahim Ismaa'il had stayed in the 1920s (see history section above). The story revealed the racial tensions that arose from conditions after the war and the plight of Somalis who thought that Cardiff was a safe place to stay.

The students kept a timeline throughout the enquiry (an example is shown in figure 7.2), noting key developments in the story of the British Empire as well as events in the Somali stories. The chronology would help them appreciate aspects of continuity and change through the enquiry. The class learned about the history of Somalia's successful decolonization after British and Italian rule, witnessing Africa's first democratic transition of government after independence in 1960. The subsequent dictatorship of Barré was also examined, and the internal strife that followed his entanglement with Cold War politics in the 1980s, causing more migration to Britain. Through the lives of the Cardiff elders, students build up a narrative of the push-and-pull factors behind Somali migration and settlement in Britain, and can respond with empathy to the histories of such marginalized citizens. The final lesson included discussions about Mo Farah, a highly successful Somali-born British athlete, who illustrates the concepts of assimilation and autonomy in different dimensions of his life and work. Using three television clips, we showed him in various contexts, including parading with the Union Jack after victory in an Olympic race – but only after he had touched the ground in prostration to Allah. As time passes, Farah's story develops and gains complexity, since he now trains for much of the year in the USA, adding to his story of migration and globalization.

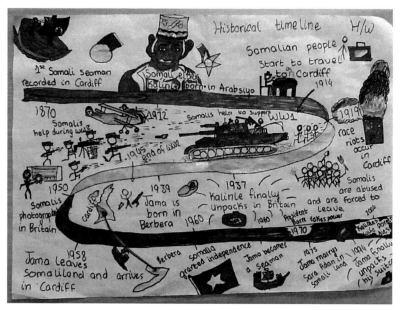

Figure 7.2: A student's timeline for Mohamoud Kalinle and Jama (authors' image)

Table 7.1 Outline of the seven-lesson enquiry on British Somali history

Why did Somali people finally decide to unpack their suitcases in Britain?

Lesson 1: How did Somali men connect with the world of Cardiff in 1950?

Summary: The initial interruption of the psyche and intrigue of the enquiry is the presence of Somali men in Cardiff praying in a mosque in 1950, long before most imagine that they were present in the UK. The idea of Somali people often being nomads in their homeland is compared with the idea of being settlers, and these notions are linked with the key substantive concepts of autonomy and assimilation. Students consider how the Somalis might have had dual loyalties and identities in Cardiff in 1950. Finally, the suitcase metaphor is introduced, along with the idea of the *packed* and *unpacked* suitcase and the enquiry question.

Activities include: Exploring the picture of Somalis at prayer in 1950; students are only told the year, and discuss: Where is this? What are the men doing? Who are these men? They then study the picture of the four men in the living room, all dressed in Western-style suits and ties, and one man sitting on the floor playing a tambourine. The sense of dual identities emerges from the discussions about the pictures. The discussion about nomads and settlers, autonomy and assimilation, sets up the suitcase metaphor. Students need to write down key definitions throughout. Finish with a discussion about the difference in the meaning of a suitcase to a nomad and a settler, ending with the enquiry question.

Lesson 2: What factors have been significant in the development of Somali society and culture?

Summary: This lesson consolidates the ideas of assimilation and autonomy and explores the geopolitical and social background of Somalia and its people. The complexity of Somali identity emerges from studying a map and considering the pull of the African continent versus the Indian Ocean, and the widespread adoption of Islam in the Near East. The concepts of continuity and change are considered in relation to assimilation and autonomy.

Activities include: Role-playing as a Somali man with his suitcase at Paddington station in 1950, being interviewed about his arrival and outlook in Britain; he's bound for Cardiff. Students come up with questions to ask him. They could also study a further photograph of Somalis in Cardiff showing four young men in a house café. Consider: How far do they look as if they have 'made themselves at home'? Then consider the location focus for Somalia: continent (Africa) and ocean (Indian), discussing different features. Students discuss the importance of trading across the Indian Ocean, and what that could bring in terms of culture as well as traded goods. The three key elements are Sunni Islam, the sarong and the suitcase.

Lesson 3: Why did Somalis first come to Britain?

Summary: The integration of Somalia into the British Empire illustrates globalization and imperialism in the nineteenth century. Britain's imperial connection and the turning-point represented by the Suez Canal, opened in 1869, is considered, through the presence of a Somali seaman in Cardiff by 1870. This then connects with the involvement of Somali seamen in the First World War, ending with the Cardiff race riot of 1919, showing the racial tensions that began to emerge in the UK.

Activities include: Students begin a timeline, working backward from 1950 where the lessons began. They annotate a large map of the British Empire from the late nineteenth century, showing the significance of India as Britain's 'Jewel in the Crown of Empire', the trade routes and the building of the shortcut at the Suez Canal. The connection with British imperialism is shown to continue in the First World War, with a photograph of Somali seamen on board a British ship off Singapore in 1915. Finally, considering an extract from Ibrahim Ismaa'il's autobiography in which he describes the 1919 Cardiff race riots, students compose a short radio broadcast from the months just after the riots, considering doubts that people may then have had about migration and assimilation.

Lesson 4: Why were so many Somalis pushed away from their homeland in the late twentieth century?

Summary: Students explore the idea that migration is a response to both push and pull factors. The early history of independent Somalia showed great success in democratic politics, with an almost unique democratic transfer of power for an African state in 1968. The dictatorship of the military leader Barré brought benefits and costs to the country; these are explored. But then Somalia became embroiled in Cold War politics and the civil war began. In 1991 Barré's government collapsed as a result of the war, and a lot of Somalis decided to emigrate.

Activities include: Students watch a video clip that sheds light on events after Somalia's independence, noting the encouragements and challenges of the 1960s. After hearing an explanation of the Barré coup, students read short statements about Barré's tenure and decide whether these represent failures or successes of leadership. They then discuss: 'Which one of these points do you think would be most important in encouraging people to leave Somalia?'

Lessons 5 & 6: What can the life stories of Somali elders tell us about Somali migration to Britain?

Summary: The stories of the Somali elders of Cardiff provide plenty of material for students to consolidate the concepts behind the migration of the Somalis to the UK. The pictures and stories can be analysed in terms of work, family and appearance, and the notions of assimilation and autonomy. Two of the elders, Mohamoud Kalinle and Mohamud Jama Mohamed, are compared: the older Kalinle, from a very traditional Somali background, married a Welsh woman in Cardiff, whilst Jama came as a teenager and worked in a coal mine before going to sea, then went back to Somalia to marry and have children (whilst still himself based in Wales), and brought them to Cardiff only when the civil war began. There should be discussion about each of the elders' possible answer to the enquiry question.

Activities include: The lives of elders are displayed on single sheets of A4, preferably in colour and laminated. The lessons should begin with one picture, perhaps Kalinle's, and discussion of when this man 'unpacked' in Britain. Then the students can use tables to record details about some of the elders. Finish with a book proposal submission for the autobiography of one of the elders, showing why their story is interesting and significant for British people, of both Somali and non-Somali backgrounds.

Lesson 7: How did Somali people develop their identities through migration to Britain?

Summary: This optional lesson introduces some complex substantive concepts showing how the migration stories of British Somalis connect to global dimensions of world development, depending on the capacity of the class. The further elder story of Hussein Abdi is complex and full of ambiguities: coming from a privileged background in pre-independence British Somaliland, he amassed considerable wealth to support a very successful family and illustrates global dimensions in many ways. Mo Farah is our final example of a migrant Somali in Britain, and his identity as a world athlete is also a good focus for considering the global dimensions and enquiry question. The ideas of assimilation and autonomy are considered in relation to Farah.

Activities include: The introduction of three global dimensions: imperialism, postcolonialism and globalization. These are discussed and defined, and students then consider how the issues of the enquiry lessons relate to these themes. Students examine the story of Hussein Abdi, considering when and why Hussein 'unpacked his suitcase'. Discuss how the stories of the Somali elders mention certain influences on their sense of identity. Then show the three Mo Farah clips, and ask the students to discuss the question: 'From what you can see in these videos, how has Mo Farah developed his ideas of identity since coming to Britain?' The enquiry finishes with a written response to the enquiry question, which could be presented in the form of an annotated timeline, to include details of the lives of at least two of the elders, as well as wider historical events and aspects.

Transforming the learning and teaching of British Somali history

The most heartening response to our work on British Somali history came in George Mitchell School, right at the beginning of the research and development period. A group of white working-class boys had been sat together in a group in one of the Year 9 classes, thoroughly engaged in the one-hour pilot lesson. After the lesson they told their history teacher that they had really appreciated the lesson because it 'had taught us about our friends'. Too often the value of multicultural history has been presented in terms of individual identities and the importance of including particular hidden histories to boost the self-esteem of that heritage group. However, these boys reminded us that community identity could have plurality that means the hidden histories of one ethnic minority community can engage the wider community in appreciation of their nation's development.

However, the contribution of history to students' identities is not straightforward, especially when deep-rooted prejudices and stereotypes are exposed in everyday life. The most surprising, and indeed alarming, response to the enquiry into British Somali history came from Somali students. The underachievement of Somali students has been acknowledged as a serious problem within the London school system (Kahin, 1997). The problems these students face are numerous and well documented, foremost amongst them being a lack of belonging to wider British society, a feeling that is closely connected to self-esteem (Ma, 2003). We assumed that our work on British Somali history would make a positive contribution to the self-esteem of Somali students. But our simplistic notions were exploded when we found that the most disengaged students in the classes that studied the enquiry were Somali boys, who often adopted a sceptical and disengaged stance in the lessons. More surprising still was that these same students expressed satisfaction with the lessons when they were over.

When we questioned them about this, they explained that at first they feared the lessons would expose aspects of their people's history that could subject them to ridicule, or that they might not be proud of, and it was only at the end of the enquiry that they were reassured that this was not the case. We think that the root of their reticence lay in the portrayal of Somalis in the media: images of piracy, unrest and famine. The students' anxieties were probably compounded by the way in which the lessons were constructed in order to maintain intrigue and allow for development through the staged disclosure of information. They might have been worried about what the next slide would show: a hostage-taking pirate? A malnourished child, perhaps, or some war-torn landscape? Although we had avoided current news items, the students already had the 'familiar' pejorative ideas in their heads, so just by presenting Somali people in a lesson we risked opening up a Pandora's box of social and cultural anxieties. We still want to trust in the power of the initial positive images to interrupt the psyche and get students to challenge contemporary stereotypes and myths, but we might consider the idea of including an antagonist early on, as we did with Hegel and Fairclough in other enquiries (see Chapters 3 and 4), so the students, particularly those of Somali heritage, can be sure that the enquiry will tackle those injustices.

Many students did testify to the power of this enquiry to interrupt their psyches and present them with surprisingly positive stories of Somalis in Britain. Parvez, an Asian student in a West London multiracial boys' comprehensive, talked about wrestling with misconceptions about these migrants:

> The British people they went, I think we learned about it that they went and got Black people as slaves, and then I thought that the Black community was populated and there was some Somalians, and because they went to Africa and got some people and brought it to Britain, I thought that it would be more because of the slave trade that there would be more Somalians, that escaped or the ones that are like settled.
>
> (Parvez, Year 8 student)

The dominance of slavery as the motif of Black history of any kind was not surprising, particularly since the British Somali enquiry was the only Black history topic these students studied apart from the transatlantic slave trade. Parvez testified to the power of the personal stories of Somali elders in Britain to engage students in thinking about the history of migration, and offering positive models of character and aspiration:

> It surprised me because they came all the way, we learned that they went from Somaliland all the way to Dover and then came to Cardiff and I think we learned that Kalinle, he went and sold their boat and then went, like it fascinated me: they wanted to find more jobs, and they wanted to do it so bad, that they sold their own stuff to do it, and they knew they were in a risk, because there were loads of bad people in that time, like some of the British people could have come and took over their ship and they could have just had nothing ... but he didn't care about the

consequences and he was just trying to help his family … and I like the fact that he went to look for a job and didn't just stay there and wait for a job to come to him, he went to look, and also that he tried to blend in, like assimilate with the British and didn't just stay there and let life happen.

(Parvez, Year 8 student)

Parvez was not known for being engaged in his history lessons, but he found the enquiry approach to history much more compelling than the usual transmissive pedagogy (see Chapter 1). He appears to have identified with the story of Kalinle, a man whom he would at first have assumed to be descended from slaves. Like most of his class, Parvez's heritage lies outside Britain, and the British Somali history enquiry has engaged him in thinking about migration stories and the concepts of assimilation and autonomy. The British Somali enquiry confirms that notions of Britishness and social cohesion can be enhanced through the exploration of hidden British stories that confront the injustices perpetuated by myths and stereotypes.

Chapter 8

Transforming Black history in teaching: Three case studies

8.1: Challenging historical fear and loathing: Black history instruction in the United States

Jenice L. View

In 1933 Dr Carter G. Woodson, the 'father of Black history', defined 'the miseducation of the Negro' in terms of the cultural indoctrination of African Americans into a position of dependency and servitude, and he charged teachers and scholars with the task of correcting for bad historical information that reinforced second-class citizenship (Woodson, 2009). In the opening chapter, Mohamud and Whitburn articulate 'a strong emphasis on trust in relation to the work of teachers in the world of education' in the UK. This is less true of the situation in the United States as the federal and state governments impose curricula, and thereby foster pedagogical restrictions on classroom practice. The US emphasizes the new Taylorism (Au, 2011), consisting of high-stakes standardized tests that serve as the sole measures of student knowledge and achievement and, in many cases, of teacher skill and employability. Language arts and mathematics are the most fiercely tested subject areas, but social studies and history are heavily scrutinized for signs of failure to conform to narratives of American exceptionalism and for promoting political agendas perceived to be extreme (Haq, 2014; Heitin, 2015; Lerner, 2015; Palos and McGinnis, 2012). The resulting miseducation includes curricular content that encodes a single perspective of a historical moment or person, or content that implies that a person is universally perceived to be heroic or infallible. 'Doing justice to history' would contest this kind of miseducation, but there is a question of who is responsible for correcting misinformation and the process for doing so. This case study examines efforts in the United States to teach Black history, efforts in the state of Mississippi to use the state history framework as a corrective measure and recommendations for improving teacher agency in delivering this important content.

Traditional Black history instruction in the United States

While African-American historical content has been used in public schools since the late nineteenth century, its purposes and ownership have transformed over time (View, 2013). Initially, people newly freed from slavery used their segregated public classrooms to tell jubilant and heroic stories as a subversive act against the rising policies of white supremacy eventually encoded in the 1896 US Supreme Court decision in *Plessy v. Ferguson,* which supported 'separate but equal' public facilities, including schools (US Supreme Court, 1896). After Dr Carter G. Woodson's establishment of Negro History Week in 1926, African-American teachers and scholars developed classroom materials for use in these racially segregated schools, aiming to inspire African-American children with stories of Black innovations in American history, technology and the arts, and tales of military victories, all intended to demonstrate their worthiness for equal citizenship.

By the 1970s, following the social and political upheavals of the modern Civil Rights Movement, Black History Month became part of the official curricula for government-sanctioned celebrations of African-American contributions to American nation building and socio-economic advancement. It adopted a 'heroes and holidays' approach first critiqued by James Banks (1993) and challenged by Lee *et al.* (1998) and others in practice. By 2005, a national survey of high-school students of all races and ethnicities indicated that the top three most 'famous Americans' were African Americans – Dr Martin Luther King Jr, Rosa Parks and Harriet Tubman (Wineburg and Monte-Sano, 2008). Yet, with the narrowing of all public school curricula, textbook versions of historical content addressing the presence of African Americans on the US landscape have been reduced to resemble this popular T-shirt: 'Rosa [Parks] sat, so Martin [Luther King Jr] could stand, so [President] Obama could run, so our children can fly' (quoted in Mosely, 2008).

The fear and loathing of Black history persists into the twenty-first century. In a 2014 study, teachers were given the opportunity to make curricular choices and explain their rationales for a hypothetical unit on the modern Civil Rights Movement (Swalwell *et al.,* 2014). Both pre-service and in-service teachers, African American and white, of all grade levels, made 'safe' choices that avoided discussions about enslavement, institutional racism and extra-legal violence despite the indisputable fact that this social, political and economic movement was explicitly intended to dismantle institutional racism in the United States.

Black history projects in Mississippi

The state of Mississippi provides a good centrepiece for teaching the history of African Americans: its reputation as a ferociously resistant land for African-American freedom has been well documented by Civil Rights veterans and scholars. McComb, Mississippi, is a particularly rich location for unearthing and teaching the histories of the young people who were the intellectuals, strategists and front-line activists in the 1950s and 1960s, seeking to transform Mississippi into a multicultural democracy (CivilRightsVeterans.org, n.d.). Among these activists were young people from the Student Nonviolent Coordinating Committee (SNCC) who proposed that the legacy of the systematic under- and mis-education of all of Mississippi's students, and the history of woefully underfunded schools in African-American communities, be addressed by Freedom Schools, subsequently run by the Council of Federated Organizations during the 1964 Freedom Summer campaign for voting rights.

More than 50 years later, Mississippi consistently ranks near the bottom of most national measures of academic achievement and performance (Education Week, 2015) and among the states with the largest relative population of African Americans (World Heritage Encyclopedia, 2015). In 2006, the *Mississippi Truth Project* was instrumental in securing state legislation that mandates the teaching of civil and human rights history in all Mississippi K–12 classrooms (Mississippi Senate Bill 2718). The intention was to formalize the desire for 'Mississippi's central role in the civil rights struggle [to be] taught as a beacon of hope for all of our citizens' (ibid.: Section 1). As the site of SNCC's first attempt at voting rights organization and 'freedom education', McComb was an ideal laboratory for gauging the power of a civil rights and labour history curriculum in transforming African-American and white students and teachers.

Teaching for Change, a non-profit organization based in Washington, DC, which co-published *Putting the Movement Back into Civil Rights Teaching* (Menkart *et al.*, 2004), was in 2005 invited by the superintendent of McComb public schools to help create a curriculum with a focus on local history, and to provide professional development to classroom teachers in the use of interactive and enquiry-based pedagogies. Since 2005, Teaching for Change has worked with the McComb schools and other districts throughout Mississippi to serve this mission. The resulting US history curriculum spanned the period from 1491 to the present. Teacher professional development workshops focused on enquiry pedagogy and dispositions, age-appropriate strategies for addressing racial identity and student activism and interdisciplinary instructional strategies. Students and teachers, African American and white, began making public presentations locally and nationally about the value of teaching and learning history through a new lens.

A three-year school-based project funded by the W.K. Kellogg Foundation, titled *Community of Promise: Building strong schools and neighborhoods through history, activism, and collaboration*, reported in 2015. This project had the objective of '[ensuring] quality education for all students in McComb, Mississippi, by finalizing and implementing the civil rights curriculum with an emphasis on early childhood education' (W.K. Kellogg Foundation, 2015). An offshoot was the McComb Legacies after-school project:

> a youth leadership program that provided middle and high school youth with the opportunity to learn about, document, and share their local civil rights movement and labor history. Participants also use the lessons learned from history to examine and take action to improve their world today.
>
> (ibid.)

With the support of school district and community adults, McComb Legacies students gathered additional oral histories from 'working people of all races, women, and young people that document how they have strived for equity in labor, civics, education, economics, and the arts' (McComb Legacies, 2011). Students created a website, as well as films, plays and presentations based on local history; they entered state and national History Day competitions and engaged in discussions about how to improve their community through civic engagement and contemporary voting rights. Participating students gained a great deal of historical knowledge, self-confidence and leadership skills as a result of the project.

Nevertheless, a 2014 report of the Southern Poverty Law Center, *Teaching the Movement*, which evaluated teaching about the Civil Rights Movement in schools nationwide, gave the state of Mississippi a ranking of C (52 per cent), meaning that the state had 'significant additional work to do to ensure that students have a satisfactory, comprehensive picture of the civil rights movement' (Southern Poverty Law Center, 2014). The report noted that, compared with other states, Mississippi standards 'do an excellent job of sequencing content across grades … as well as linking the civil rights movement to current events' (ibid.: 80). However, the states that earned an A (scoring at least 80 per cent) generally had higher expectations than Mississippi in terms of content proficiency and helping students develop a comprehensive understanding of the Movement. The report does not speak to the centuries of African Americans in Mississippi, but expresses the need to place the Civil Rights Movement in a broader context, in terms of both its geography (it is not merely a Southern history) and its demography (it is not merely an African-American history). It also criticized the fact that many of the materials and resources used were Mississippi-centric, although many would argue that the Civil Rights Movement as it manifested in Mississippi was a significant driver for the national movement.

In 2014, Teaching for Change received additional funds from the W.K. Kellogg Foundation to establish a summer professional development institute, the Mississippi Teacher Fellowship on Civil Rights Movement and Labor History. The purpose of this two-year fellowship programme is 'to build a sustainable statewide learning community of classroom language arts, social studies, and history teachers in grades 6–12 for teaching hands-on, inquiry based US history through the lens of race and class in Mississippi history' (McComb Legacies, 2011) During the one-week institute scheduled for summer 2015, and through follow-up seminars with scholars and with civil rights and labour veterans, teachers will develop and share lessons and other resources over the course of the school year.

Justice and Black history in the US

Both Dr Carter G. Woodson and the Southern Poverty Law Center observed that a lack of strong teaching materials and official endorsement hamper efforts to incorporate Black history into the US historical canon. The recent evidence of punitive actions against teachers who deviate from orthodoxy or whose students fail to score well on standardized measures of achievement would strike fear into anyone seeking a long career as a classroom instructor. Schools are inherently conservative agencies of the state that do not intend for students to transform the conditions and the content of their own learning, or, in a word, school itself. Seeking to do justice to history will lead us to approach different facets of the notion of justice, including procedural justice, which would ensure that students follow the disciplinary processes acknowledged as being inherent to the work of historians; a veracious justice that would be concerned with moving closer to greater knowledge about what actually happened in the past, why things happened and how far change happened; restorative justice, which would bring back histories that had been – wilfully or unwittingly – neglected and hidden; and correctional justice, which seeks to address errors, falsehoods and myths that have persisted in interpretations of the past.

Procedural justice

Processes that would enable our students to do greater justice to the work of the history classroom include examining multiple accounts and perspectives on any given historical event or person; engaging in rigorous analysis of primary sources; engaging in a thorough investigation of the provenance of the primary sources to make sense of the origins and purposes of the sources; using maps, timelines, cultural artefacts, texts and images to place primary sources in a context; and making connections between the claims one makes in a historical argument and the evidence to support those claims (Historical Thinking Matters, n.d.; TeachingHistory.org, n.d.). Additional aspects of historical thinking include understanding the ways that people and places change over time, exploring debates about the various causes of historical events, embracing the inherent complexity of historical events and people, and the unsettling idea of contingency – that is to say, appreciating that things could just as easily have turned out differently in the past and that the future is up for grabs based on contemporary human actions (Andrews and Burke, 2007). At a minimum, teachers and students engaged in historical thinking would necessarily examine the state, community and individual powers governing curricular choices, even as they investigate the curricular materials they are expected to master.

Veracious justice

A more nuanced, complex and historically accurate history of African Americans that helps to establish not only a greater sense of truth about the past, but also a 'felt difficulty' (Dewey, 1933; Barton and Levstik, 2004) for students and teachers, will acknowledge the ways in which white supremacist ideology is encoded in the DNA of what became the United States. The history of the current residents of the USA is the history of raced, classed and gendered individuals in a landscape that was multicultural at its inception. It includes the pre-enslavement histories of continental Africans and the cultural legacies brought across on the Middle Passage to the New World from 20 different regions of the African continent, 45 distinct ethnic groups and 173 city-states. It illuminates the intersections with the histories of the estimated 100 million indigenous peoples representing more than 200 different cultural groups, including Alaska Natives, that in 1491 populated what is now known as North and South America. It analyses the differences between the English enslavement of Africans at the Jamestown settlement in Virginia in 1607 and the practices of the Spanish in Central and South American begun nearly 100 years earlier in the seven distinct civilizations and cultures of Mexico and Central America, including the Olmecs, Mayans and Aztecs, plus the indigenous peoples of Puerto Rico and of the lands in the Caribbean that later became US territories. A more veraciously just history will also include the many journeys that made Asians and Pacific Islanders into Americans.

Restorative justice

Among the most egregious omissions in US history teaching are the centuries of resistance and alliances, including with poor and working-class whites, against slavery, neo-slavery, extra-legal violence and segregation (Baptist, 2014; Blackmon, 2008; Horne, 2014). In addition there are the histories of the immigrations, the annexations and imperialist acts that created what we now call the United States. For example, nineteenth-century Britain and Spain enslaved people from China, India and the Philippines to work in the Caribbean and South America. Subsequently, a large number of Chinese came voluntarily to the US to participate in the Gold Rush and to escape the British dominance of China following the Opium War. Japanese workers were recruited to work on Hawaiian colonial plantations, and eventually migrated to the mainland United States. People from Pacific Island nations, such as Native Hawaiians, Filipinos, Guamanians and Samoans, and East Asians and Southeast Asians, including Koreans, Vietnamese and Cambodians, eventually became part of the US population, sometimes by choice, sometimes as a result of US imperialism and war. Dr Carter G. Woodson's own years in the Philippines (1903–7) as a US Government school supervisor immediately after the defeat of Filipino revolutionaries in the Philippine–American War (1899–1902) surely complicate our understanding of Woodson's development of Negro History Week.

Correctional justice

The notion of correctional justice gives a deeper explanation of *why* wars, immigrations, enslavements, resistances and uprisings occurred in history. Moreover, it challenges approaches to history that single out the individual (usually white) 'Great Man' as the most important agent of change. Even most histories of the Civil Rights Movement ignore the many women, children and organizations that acted alongside better-known figures to transform history. The scholarship of Black women like Clark Hine (1994), Giddings (2007) and Hull *et al.* (1982) offer new ways of understanding how Black history was made also by women.

Finally, social studies and history teachers have a unique opportunity to help all children, at all grade levels, to explore their racial identities in a positive and constructive environment. This understanding includes the economic dimensions of these raced identities over time. The exploration and development of healthy identities (racialized and otherwise) are part of the task of using social studies and history to socialize children as citizens of a multicultural democracy.

Teacher agency

A major emphasis in US history courses, at least during Black History Month, is the Civil Rights Movement. The Civil Rights Movement is a national, not a regional, issue. It has lessons for students beyond those in the South. In the words of noted civil rights historian Taylor Branch, 'If you're trying to teach people to be citizens, teach them about the civil rights movement' (Southern Poverty Law Center, 2014: 9). Yet Black history is larger and longer than what is considered the modern Civil Rights Movement. I would argue that if we are trying to teach people to be US and global citizens, we must teach them the histories of all of the people inhabiting the United States. The benefits to children of colour may seem obvious, in that their histories and cultures would have voice and standing in classroom materials. In addition, empirical evidence suggests that white students develop stronger social, political and academic skills by virtue of negotiating multicultural curricula and classrooms (e.g. Hughes *et al.*, 2006; Tegeler, 2013), despite an earlier 2006 report of the US Commission on Civil Rights arguing that there was a lack of hard data to support the value of racial and ethnic diversity in schools.

Throughout history the best teachers, regardless of personal political ideology, have never allowed state-approved materials to be their sole resource, have never been conformists, have never allowed fear to deter them from teaching complex truths and have always loved their students. Fear and loathing as expressed by uncritically championing the idea of American exceptionalism are not part of the repertoire of master US history teachers. Deep inquiry, even in the early grades, can create a stronger attachment to history content and the dramatic stories of our nation than the flat, cardboard offerings in most classrooms. And, for now, it is up to the courageous classroom teachers to embrace the task of teaching authentic Black history.

8.2: Student and teacher activism and the pursuit of justice in the history curriculum at George Mitchell School

Martin Spafford

'Why?' – Summer 1995

'Why?' started at George Mitchell, an 11–16 mixed comprehensive school in East London, UK, as a response to action by children. In 1995 a Year 7 (age 11) Somali boy had been excluded for showing a knife when threatened by an older boy who called him 'a stupid refugee'. His classmates were furious, saying the school should have understood the boy's background. They successfully persuaded the school authorities to let their friend return to school and were now demanding to know more. *Why were children refugees? How were they being treated and how should we receive them?* I knew the importance of respecting young people's desire to understand, and it was clear that we needed to explore these questions. With the permission of the six refugee children in the class, we decided to launch a project, known as 'Why?'. Our aim was to help the class understand historical, political and social contexts for the fact that more than 10 per cent of their fellow students were from refugee families. We wanted them to have an opportunity to become active citizens and promote social justice then and there by engaging with history and current politics.

As they listened to speakers and watched video clips, the class soon decided they wanted to make films and create a performance piece. Every single member of the class took part. In one film the boy tells the story that so moved his friends to action:

> They broke the door down ... they took our phones and money and bombed the house. I couldn't do nothing – they'd got big guns. My dad was already dead. People ran away ... I saw lots of bodies lying in the corridors and all the houses bombed and all the people were crying and running around ... I was feeling scared and angry.
>
> (Year 7 student, George Mitchell School)

Another film explores how refugees are treated by the British state. While students are in front of Parliament interviewing a refugee who had been beaten up while in detention, a government minister, Jeremy Hanley, walks past. The students say, 'We'll interview him!' and start quizzing him with direct off-the-cuff challenges:

> Sam: When refugees come to this country they get beaten about and taken to detention centres!
>
> Jeremy Hanley: Well, the United Kingdom has got a very good record on receiving refugees ... but if there are those who are trying to defraud the system, obviously they must be rooted out and returned.
>
> Sam: Do you think Britain will keep selling arms to different countries?
>
> Hanley: Yes, as long as those countries don't use the arms for bad purposes ... we do sell to those we believe have a right to self-protection.
>
> [Hanley leaves and the students talk to camera]
>
> Sam: ... This country is still selling arms and they are killing each other and he knows that but he is still willing to sell arms to them.
>
> Wasim: They are killing people and they don't want to take refugees!
>
> (Interview with Jeremy Hanley MP by
> Year 7 students, George Mitchell School)

The final content was entirely the students'. In the films and performance, as well as a class discussion of racism, they argue passionately about politics and history, and show the depth of knowledge and understanding in children that we only uncover in schools if we stop seeing them as empty vessels to be filled, and recognize the wisdom and experience already filling them. People heard about the project and the students were asked to perform at schools and universities and outside Parliament. Four years later, aged 16, they were still presenting their Year 7 project with pride.

'Why?' had a huge effect on my practice as a teacher, leading to many other projects based on similar principles. The classroom has to be a place where we tackle difficult issues – adults and children together – because they have to be faced, and from where we take them into the wider world, not only imaginatively and intellectually but in reality. We should never underestimate the intelligence, creativity and sense of solidarity of children – but if we don't allow it space we'll never see it and its roots may shrivel. After 'Why?' I have tried always to say yes to a request from a child or to an offer of a learning experience that may break boundaries.

The students still affirm how 'Why?' affected them. Sixteen years later five of them met to discuss its impact on their adult lives:

> Kemi: 'Why?' was really about respect ... serious political issues of that day, that are still apparent now, and twelve-year-olds were talking about it, and were passionate about it ... As a young person you need to articulate yourself and be allowed to know that your voice is actually valued.

> Riz: 'Why?' had a major influence on my life and how I saw people. Today I was actually filling out an application form and it said *What was your biggest achievement?* And I actually wrote about 'Why?'... how we all stuck together as a team and carried ourselves forward and in the end that was the most beautiful thing that ever happened to me.

> (Former 'Why?' participants Kemi and Riz)

'Why?' was possible thanks to George Mitchell School, Stella East, Hugh Meteyard and Anna Hermann of LEAP Theatre Workshop.

Journey to Justice LIVE (2015)

Learning from history can inspire people to feel able to take action for change: studying the achievements and setbacks of the past can help us in our own struggles for social justice. A more recent project, Journey to Justice, has grown from a belief in this idea and led us to work with two groups of vulnerable young people in an East London school. One group, from Years 9 and 10, were all marginalized in school and involved in daily struggles in their own lives. They had no previous involvement in enrichment programmes, tended to be seen by teachers as 'disruptive' and were not used to being heard. The second group consisted of children from Years 7, 8 and 9 who were fairly isolated socially and some of whom had experienced bullying. Our aim was for the views of these students – who had never had such an opportunity – to be articulated and heard. Both groups would learn about past struggles for justice and action for change. We wanted the young people to engage with stories from the past they could relate to, so we first showed them clips from the 'Why?' project: they saw child activists like themselves in the same school 20 years earlier. They then investigated four cases of children taking action for change: the Burston School strike; Ruby Bridges, a black primary school girl entering an all-white school in New Orleans in 1960; the Soweto students' uprising in South Africa in 1976; and Malala Yousafzai standing up for girls' education in Pakistan in the present day.

We began to coach them in public speaking and took them to a preview screening of the film *Selma*, where four of them spoke alongside an MP, a baroness and a lord. We looked together at protest music in the USA, UK, Africa and Latin America from the 1960s to today. An invitation from Lord Herman Ouseley to address a meeting at the House of Lords two months after the start of the project was an important moment in the project: this was a clear objective in the 'real' world outside school for young people who had never addressed an audience in their lives. We encouraged them to think about issues of concern to them that they might pursue. At the House of Lords they described one issue of great concern to them: gun and knife crime and the drift into gangs. A housing rights activist from Cardiff visited the group of students and described the process involved in creating a movement. They began sharing ideas about what changes were possible that would improve their lives and also described their work in school assemblies. Some were writing poems that addressed their own struggles, triggered by the lives in the past they were hearing about and inspired by contemporary and past writers, including Alexandra's powerful account of what it was like to be bullied about her size, which had been unlocked in response to the story of Ruby Bridges. The young people were central. Back in school, the project continued. The students have decided that they will campaign to have students involved in decision-making over pupil exclusions. They will meet a panel of senior staff to present their ideas and will do so on their own. Their first meeting with the headteacher and deputy was successful; the head wrote back to tell them he was:

> very impressed by the quality of the presentation and the research you had completed in preparation for the meeting with us. It was good to see statistical research underpinning your claims and I thought the real life examples worked well in terms of setting the context for the discussion.... I like the idea of a Student Advisory Panel.
>
> (Head teacher, George Mitchell School, 2015)

He asked them to consider a series of questions about aims and structure, to which they are, at the time of writing, responding.

JtoJ Live was possible thanks to Carrie Supple, Parul Motin, Rosaleen Lyons, Faduma Elmi, Winstan Whitter, Lord Herman Ouseley and George Mitchell School. The brief project film can be seen at http://journeytojustice. org.uk/projects/journey-to-justice-all-over-the-uk

8.3: Case studies of history beyond the classroom: The South African history educational visit and Black History Month celebrations at St Mary's High School, Hendon, UK

Michelle Hussain

St Mary's was an inner-city comprehensive Church of England secondary school, the closure of which was announced in 2012, with a diverse student demographic that reflected how fast London's population was and still is changing. The history department had a strong collective belief in developing a history curriculum that was culturally relevant and that included discussion as an integral aspect of pedagogy, whereby students could access quite complex themes confidently (Ladson-Billings, 1995; Pankhania, 1994). Teachers often had to work hard to secure their own knowledge and understanding of histories they had never studied themselves. One example was a Year 8 scheme of work on early African history in the oral tradition of storytelling, where lessons were taught without any writing (Whitburn *et al.*, 2012). St Mary's students did not see the study of multicultural history as an add-on (Apple, 2004); they appreciated it as an integral part of their regular study of history. They could also access the curriculum via their most powerful tool – talk and discussion – and this became a central learning mode in lessons. Students often commented on the importance of being able to voice their ideas and opinions on history during lessons (Whitburn *et al.*, 2012).

One very important aspect of the history department's work in recent years was the annual celebration of Black History Month. It was one of the first projects the history department embarked upon when the school was restructured under new leadership in 2004. The department wanted the planning to come from students, and chose to work with a group of Year 9 students that included some who were very disaffected with school in general, but maintained an interest in their history lessons. The students were keen to contribute ideas and participate in the planning and organization of a range of celebratory activities, including two exhibition nights showcasing student work produced in lessons, drama, music and T-shirts with a Black History Month St Mary's logo designed by the group. The image showed an upright hand cradling a ball on which was written a quote from Bob Marley's song 'Buffalo Soldier': 'If you know your history then you will know where you are coming from.' Over the years students wrote and performed many moving raps and songs, and created many pieces of drama and art for the celebrations. The annual celebrations started in 2005 and became more ambitious each year. Each was contextually different and unique, depending on the theme of the event and the student group involved in the planning. A sixth-form conference was launched in the second year of the celebrations and included talks from St Mary's alumni who had gone to university to study aspects of Black history. Three of them went on to become history teachers themselves. HYBO – the 'History of Black Origin' – was the name the department gave to the celebrations from 2007, inspired by the MOBO (Music of Black Origin) awards. The presentation of 'HYBO awards' for special contributions to Black history and the school began in the same year. These became highly sought after; one student even had the ambition to win all of them – which he eventually did.

South Africa and the HYBO of 2009

Early HYBO themes had explored the anniversary of the abolition of the slave trade, the anniversary of Ghana's independence and the history of the Caribbean. The department eventually chose South Africa as its theme for 2009 because of the country's long struggle for peace, justice and equality, and because it seemed a natural choice after a transformational sixth-form educational visit to the country the previous February. As part of their A-Level programme of study, the students were taught a module on the rise of African nationalism and the department undertook the journey to Johannesburg to enable students to experience the historical transformation and remembrance that was taking place in the New South Africa.

Over the years, I had developed a special relationship with South Africa as a country. I had taken three groups of students on trips before 2009 and had seen changes over the years. It felt like taking students to a living history experience, as racial divisions were clearly still visible and still determined the way most people lived. The students, who came from London, a multiracial city, were always amazed to see the legacy of apartheid that still existed openly in a modern society. The visits also make me reflect on my own values as a teacher, as I visited schools where teachers provided education, love, structure and hope to students in the face of extremely challenging circumstances. In London, I always complained when the photocopier broke down or my interactive whiteboard didn't work; when reflecting on how amazing these teachers were, despite not having adequate stationery to teach with, my first-world problems seemed meaningless. South Africa was a special place and we were determined to return to London and devote time to sharing with our own school the history of that country and the communities its history has forged.

The key question and theme of this HYBO was 'When the good times lie in the future, what do you do with the grim past?' This allowed the department to acknowledge the nature of South Africa's difficult past, but also to explore the idea of the new South Africa and its exciting possibilities for a healing future. In the most ambitious HYBO conference yet, the department used the new spaces to take the audience physically through South Africa's journey. Starting in the newly built teaching space, the path went into a darker space in the school gym, where the audience encountered images and visual experiences from South Africa's apartheid past. They then moved symbolically into the light of the new South Africa through lighting candles. The conference talks and discussions were also structured chronologically, ending with speeches by students and teachers from the school we had visited in South Africa, whom we had flown over to take part in the celebrations and share their personal experiences of change and the new South Africa (see Figure 8.1, which illustrates a discussion during the 2009 HYBO). The finale was a display of Zulu dancing by two students who had travelled to visit the school from KwaZulu-Natal.

Figure 8.1: A group of British and South African guests discussing the serious issues of history at the 2009 HYBO at St Mary's Hendon (authors' image)

The impact of HYBO

Planning for the event began the previous summer and involved many meetings and student support sessions in preparation. This HYBO became a community event, with contributions from many different people who gave up their time to share their research and opinions on Black history. HYBO had a transformational impact on the students who took part, and they regularly commented on how honoured they felt to have been able to contribute: it gave them a chance to share their passion about their own history with others. André Burton, a former student of ours who helped lead the 2008 HYBO conference, said the celebration showed that 'History does not belong to one set of people and that it was relevant to everyone. It also gave them a chance to celebrate history and their own identity.'

As a teacher, I was always amazed by how willing all the people involved were to give up their time and efforts to support the event. Students' contributions always exceeded my expectations; I was especially moved when one alumna spoke in 2011 about her own history experience at the school, because she was training to be a history teacher herself. HYBO became an annual event the school was allowed to be proud of, and a reflection of the students at their best: presenting, creating, supporting, cooking, singing, rapping, dancing, researching, working hard and sharing opinions on history.

St Mary's Hendon had to begin the process of school closure in 2012. For the final HYBO, in 2012, the school was honoured to host Dame Doreen Lawrence, who spoke about her struggles for justice. Students had felt confident to present and vocalize their ideas at the conferences because of the contextual knowledge and confident understanding acquired in their studies in history lessons.

History at St Mary's was a transformational experience for the students in the history classroom as well as for those involved in HYBO. As a teacher I still feel personally honoured to have been part of such a special journey through learning, developing and sharing the history taught in lessons, as well as participating in the creation and evolution of HYBO as a school and community experience.

Chapter 9

Conclusions: The transformation of Black history in secondary schools

Our understanding of the process of educational change is based on a notion of grassroots activism; our pugilists, diggers and choreographers come from the ranks of committed practitioners, school departments and community associations, not government bodies or policy think-tanks. Our approach has been essentially pragmatic and involves developing programmes of learning that can be implemented straightaway in a school context, and can lead to immediate change in the educational experience and understanding of young people. Our historical enquiries are ready to be taught in secondary schools, and teachers in the UK, USA and South Africa have been enthusiastic to start working with these frameworks and materials. We are hopeful that deeper socio-political change can follow, and that this approach to teaching history will contribute to wider social justice.

The United Nations declared that the years 2015–24 were to be an 'International Decade for People of African Descent' (United Nations General Assembly, 2014). Under the call for 'Recognition', they declared:

> States should: Promote greater knowledge and recognition of and respect for the culture, history and heritage of people of African descent, including through research and education, and promote full and accurate inclusion of the history and contribution of people of African descent in educational curricula.
>
> (United Nations General Assembly, 2014)

The UN has placed history education firmly in the context of justice and development for Africa and the millions of people of African descent in its diasporas. The priorities of the Decade are strongly connected to issues of racism, and the declaration makes frequent references to the 2001 Durban Programme of Action, which sought to 'combat racism, racial discrimination, xenophobia and related intolerance'. This encourages us to believe that transformation in Black history education could be a part of global change and the righting of injustices for people of African descent.

If these injunctions are to effect such change, we must be prepared to think radically about the way we teach Black history and undertake a good deal of research and planning to develop new curricula and reform our pedagogy.

Jeffrey Duncan-Andrade warned of the dangers of false hopes in the field of education for Black and other minority ethnic youths in the USA, and his classification of false hopes and critical hopes can be usefully applied to the field of Black history. Two of his false hopes are 'hokey hope', which is 'a false hope informed by privilege and rooted in the optimism of the spectator who needs not suffer' (Duncan-Andrade, 2009: 183) and 'mythical hope', which is 'a profoundly ahistorical and depoliticized denial of suffering that is rooted in celebrating individual exceptions' (ibid.:184); both hopes relate to the pitfalls of popular approaches to Black history in schools. To suggest that we no longer need Black history because we are in a 'post-racial' and 'colour-blind' society is to peddle a 'hokey hope' that ignores the realities of the hegemonic power of whiteness worldwide. To present a heroic narrative of Black history, centred on Dr King and Presidents Mandela and Obama, is to project a 'mythical hope' that avoids uncomfortable and potentially controversial histories that are relevant to contemporary struggles. Duncan-Andrade presents alternative kinds of hope that don't offer easy options, and his 'Socratic hope', in particular, resonates with the opportunities we see in doing justice to Black history. This Socratic hope 'requires both teachers and students to painfully examine [their] lives and actions within an unjust society and to share the sensibility that pain may pave the path to justice' (ibid.: 187–8). We believe that certain fundamental changes in curriculum and pedagogy can be brought about through grassroots activism, and that at the heart of those changes will be a transformation of teachers of history and their students. That is how wider transformation begins.

Transforming curriculum and pedagogy

Three key features of the world of schools and education need to be transformed in order to bring about justice for Black history in the secondary classroom: justice, race and 'master' historical narratives.

Justice

Our schools are not helping teachers to do justice to Black history. Socratic hope begins to evaporate with the ascendancy in schools of a culture of teachers' accountability and their technical skills. Teachers who are driven towards the accumulation of neutral empirical facts that might demonstrate students' progress can become estranged from the very students whose future should be the focus of their quest for justice. When schools aim to neutralize their classrooms in order to 'raise standards', they are in danger of neutering their capacity to fight injustice. The eponymous character in Rousseau's *Emile* (Rousseau, 1979) learns most readily when faced with real social problems, and Emile's teacher gently guides him on the path to understanding them and to speaking and acting freely as an agent of potential change. Justice can be pursued in a history classroom that works to promote such freedom and curiosity. Students are due an inheritance from the guiding principles of the Enlightenment: liberty of thought and equality of access to the kind of history that can foster their positive involvement with social justice. In a speech in 2009 to the Royal Society of Arts the Secretary of State for Education, Michael Gove, proclaimed his belief that the purpose of education was to allow individuals to become the 'authors of their own life-stories'. He explained that the process of education should be about granting each individual an 'inheritance' of human achievement, but went on to say that the cultural experiences and knowledge that are relevant to the lives of young people should have no place in the classroom. Gove was prepared to offer young people the narrative of the Enlightenment, but he sought to deny them its principles in action.

Tackling issues of justice in the history classroom is inherently political, and if justice is taken as a key part of the processes of history students will be politicized through historical enquiry. Hannah Arendt produced a three-part typology of human activity in her political philosophy (Arendt, 1998) – *labour*, *work* and *action* – only the last of which, she argues, can fulfil the requirements of political activity. Applied to pedagogy, Arendt's ideas of *labour* and *work* could be applied to a technicist approach to pedagogy, but her notion of the higher level of *action* would bring a political dimension to the classroom, not in a partisan sense, but in the sense of political literacy, so that teachers and students are able to take an active place in the *action* of human life. *Action* is distinguished from the behavioural approaches of *labour* and *work* by its unpredictability and the promise of new diverse ideas.

A pedagogy that corresponded to the Arendtian concept of *action* would look upon the uniqueness of a class of students and their particular teacher, and see learning as a process of discovering and creating new things, particularly through the spoken participation of all those involved. A pedagogy that sees the teacher and her students as partners within the learning process, with opinions and views about that process that can be equally valid in progressing it, would be very different from notions of 'curriculum delivery' or 'model lessons'. This *democratized* classroom would be unpredictable, interactive, dialogic and flexible, rather than didactic, regimented and dominated by the teacher.

With the democratic political process come both rights and responsibilities, and our work can develop both. Students would fulfil something of the inner drive of their better natures to see fairness and righteousness prevail. This might guard against too much cynicism. Students are given a voice and agency through the enquiry process into the injustices of the past, and it is a voice with a purpose. Furthermore, students are offered the responsibility to validate their right to do justice to history through constructing accounts of neglected histories. This has aspects of honour and respect for past situations and characters, and adds a personal responsibility that would not be present in the traditional didactic classroom where students have to receive and accept the master narratives.

Race

The election in 2008 of the first African-American president of the United States was taken by some commentators as an indication that race was no longer a barrier to success, and that the world was entering a 'post-racial' era (Sugrue, 2010). There was much talk of hope, not least because of Barack Obama's autobiography *The Audacity of Hope* (Obama, 2006). It seemed we would soon see the end of Black history in this post-racial era, because race was no longer relevant. A spate of deaths of young African-American men at the hands of police officers and local volunteers in American cities, beginning with that of Trayvon Martin in 2012, showed otherwise. Within months of taking office, President Obama had to deal with an embarrassing case of racial profiling (see Chapter 2). Race was still very much a feature of American life. Racism is a troublesome concept; it is a relatively new word, having entered the arena of academic discourse in the latter half of the twentieth century. The term 'race' is used to describe a questionable set of beliefs and not undeniable facts of nature (Fredrickson, 2002). The acceptance of most reasonable people is that it was Nazi Germany's use of racial theory that produced the horrors of the Holocaust. Extensive studies into that systematic genocide have failed to explain the atrocities. The core elements of racism were not swept away by the shift in public attitudes that led to the introduction of laws designed to eradicate racial prejudice. In many countries xenophobic opposition to immigration has burgeoned alongside longer-standing racist thinking.

Racism and xenophobia are not synonymous. White European immigrants to Britain can be victims of xenophobic abuse, but would not be subject to the same injustices as those suffered by people of colour. The pernicious and pervasive social realities of the political construct of race still play a significant role in social interaction. If our goal as educators in a multiracial society and globalized world is to nurture young people and help them build confidence in themselves, then we must not ignore the historical processes that are so crucial in determining the futures of both Black people and white (Jensen, 2005; Alexander, 2010). We must give students regular opportunities to discuss and explore race in all its complexity, employing the rigour and persistence that the study of history requires. To overcome the nature and legacy of racism one must first understand it.

History teachers need to consider the narratives of their subject in relation to power relations between racialized groups. In his pioneering work on 'whiteness' W.E.B. Dubois warned against what we have called the master narratives of history teaching:

> How easy, then, by emphasis and omission to make children believe that every great soul the world saw was a white man's soul; that every great thought was a white man's thought; that every great deed the world ever did was a white man's deed; that every great dream the world ever sang was a white man's dream.
>
> (Dubois, quoted in Adler, 2009: 384)

It is important for young people to understand the part race has played in the construction of historical narratives, as well as learning the stories of Black triumphs and struggles. Culture and history are inseparable features of personhood, so teaching one people's history at the expense of others' perpetuates and legitimates oppressive social structures. Teachers need to transform the teaching of Black history: not to do so would be to damage a core aspect of the identity of people of African descent.

Master narratives and hidden histories

Our historical enquiries into Black history have interrupted the psyches of students and colleagues by bringing to light hidden histories of lives and places that confront the established master narratives that have held sway over school history curricula and common thinking about the past. Africa is far from being a 'dark continent' that depended on white Europeans to bring it into civilized modernity. At its heart is Timbuktu, a city that exemplifies ancient learning and the integration of cultures and religions, far from being a 'mysterious lost city of treasure and danger'. Robert F. Williams was not a violent 'angry Black man' to be shunned, along with Malcolm X, in the interests of a peaceful, colour-blind, co-existence in Martin Luther King Jr's 'Dream world'. Rather, Williams represents the complexity of resistance in the lives of oppressed Black people worldwide and the redundancy of many binaries in our understanding of race and history. Not all white people were oblivious to the struggles of Black people in South Africa, and the humanity of Beyers Naudé represents the possibility that people can confront the consequences of their whiteness and stand up for justice. In Claudia Jones we encountered the possibility that extreme political radicalism and deep human compassion can embolden a person to confront the oppression of Black people and transcend the confines of conformity to pursue justice and make an impact. Cardiff enriched our understanding of the long history of Britain's multicultural development, as the home of Somali people of Muslim faith working and living in diverse communities since the nineteenth century.

Yet throughout these explorations of hidden histories, the master narrative was vivid and present. Our students learned about the history of European encounters with Africa; they gathered the narrative of the traditional Civil Rights Movement; they explored the infamous event at Sharpeville as a turning-point in South African history; they understood fundamental features of twentieth-century American and British history in the Depression and Cold War backgrounds to West Indian migrant experiences; they learned how British imperial global expansion brought Somali people to the shores of the 'motherland'. These master narratives were not made redundant but instead rejuvenated by their connections to hidden histories. By combining the master narratives within the exploration of hidden histories, the enquiries give students opportunities to engage in Arendtian *action*. Working with both the new histories and the traditional narratives gives students agency in not only confronting problems with historical interpretations, but also beginning to create interpretations of their own that they can take pride in telling and developing. Dewey's 'felt difficulty' is placed firmly at the start of the learning (Barton, 2009).

The history curriculum will be transformed when we bring hidden histories such as those revealed in this book to the fore through the framework of historical enquiry. Some of the master narratives find new inspiration and energy to fashion new meanings and do justice to history. Stirred by the work of Audre Lorde (2007), scholars at University College London formed a group under the banner of 'Dismantling the Master's House' as a metaphor for the goal of scholars who are championing the overthrow of white hegemony and racism in fields of knowledge and scholarship (UCL, 2015). In challenging the master narratives we suggest that we are not *dismantling* the master's house, nor refurbishing it, but rather embarking on a fundamental *redevelopment* that could make the site fit for purpose.

Ours is a pragmatic rather than a revolutionary response, to bring about radical change at a time of nervous conservatism in Western societies. The pugilists may have wanted a more insistent stance, but in order to bring the choreographers with us, we need to ensure that teachers can meet the expectations of their institutions at the same time as transforming their history lessons. Assessment systems will still have to be satisfied, and progress measured according to school policies, but curriculum and pedagogy need to be the prime focus of development. Teachers will need to embrace change wholeheartedly if justice is to be done. How the teachers may need to change forms our final focus.

Transforming teachers

Our troika of pugilists, diggers and choreographers ultimately depend on teachers to transform Black history in schools. Some history teachers already function as choreographers who do justice to history, and their creative energies fuse with the energy of their students to forge more authentic interpretations of our past. Colleagues who aspire to choreograph the dance of history cannot be neutral: they have to identify injustice and strive to overturn it by changing what and how they teach. They need to be aware of their power to transform young people and of the damage they can cause by following an easy path through the readily available resources of the master narrative. Challenging the conventional discourses of schools will not be easy, but this lies at the heart of how we would see professionalism. Following the ideas of Ron Barnett (2008), we believe choreographers can do more than navigate the current discourse of accountability; they can, with their students, create new discourses. Working with this integrity envisions a world of justice where vigilance would replace pugilism, and hope triumph over cynicism.

Creativity within the field of Black history calls for teacher–choreographers to be politically minded and engaged, in the way that Martin Spafford describes in Chapter 8. They need to engage with the substantive fibres of historical enquiry and experience the joy of finding an invaluable source or question that fires the interest of their students within the enquiry. These sources can prompt the creative expression of the students, who in turn re-energize the teacher to mine the source again. In this way students and their teachers have the opportunity to become diggers themselves and create a new dynamic in the classroom.

Co-agency only works if there is mutual understanding and appreciation, and this calls for connection between the choreographer–teachers and their students. At the heart of connection is trust, which is why the choreographers must build informed relationships and sustain a constant dialogue with their students in the classroom. In bringing forth new interpretations of hidden histories, students need confidence in their ideas so they can speculate without fear of getting it wrong. And trust should be reciprocal, so that the students can patiently follow the teacher into realms of new knowledge on which to speculate.

The transformation of Black history needs leadership by principled teachers who will be advocates for a more just and inclusive history curriculum. They must develop their voices and be prepared to speak out for this transformation. The creative teacher has to be a pugilist, and needs skills of oratory to marshal arguments and engage in debate with others. Teachers need to transform their professional learning communities to do justice to history. A lone teacher–pugilist risks becoming reclusive. Although a lone teacher could remain hopeful and survive through interaction with students, that would not lead to a process of change in his or her fellow history teachers. Teachers who transform Black history in schools have to be connected to not only their students but also their colleagues. Regular open dialogue is needed, as in the Zulu saying *umuntu ngumuntu ngabantu* – you are an individual person only through the existence of others. This is *ubuntu*, explained by Martin Prozesky as follows:

> *Ubuntu* means that rich, personal creativity, like well-being, is only possible when individuals enjoy the supportive resources of a healthy context made up of other vigorous, fulfilled people and nature, in an ongoing process of mutual enrichment. Without that individuals wither.
>
> (Prozesky, 2009: 12)

We have been most fortunate to have enjoyed developing our work across a range of inspirational history departments. We hope the arguments and examples articulated throughout this book will spur your vital endeavours with students and colleagues to do justice to history.

References

Adler, P.S. (2009) *The Oxford Handbook of Sociology and Organization Studies: Classical foundations.* Oxford: Oxford University Press.

Alexander, M. (2010) *The New Jim Crow: Mass incarceration in the age of colorblindness.* New York: The New Press.

Allen, T.W. (2012) *The Invention of the White Race.* 2 vols. London and New York: Verso.

Andrews, T. and Burke, F. (2007) 'What does it mean to think historically?' Online. www.historians.org/publications-and-directories/perspectives-on-history/january-2007/what-does-it-mean-to-think-historically (accessed 9 June 2015).

Appiah, K.A. (1998) 'Africa: The hidden history'. *New York Review of Books*, 17 December. Online. www.nybooks.com/articles/1998/12/17/africa-the-hidden-history (accessed 5 January 2016).

Apple, M. (2004) *Ideology and Curriculum.* 3rd ed. New York and London: Routledge.

Arendt, H. (1998) *The Human Condition.* 2nd ed. Chicago: University of Chicago Press.

Atwater, D.F. (2007) 'Senator Barack Obama: The rhetoric of hope and the American Dream'. *Journal of Black Studies*, 38 (2), 121–9.

Au, W. (2011) 'Teaching under the new Taylorism: High-stakes testing and the standardization of the 21st century curriculum'. *Journal of Curriculum Studies*, 43 (1), 25–45.

Banks, J.A. (1993) 'Multicultural Education: Historical Development, Dimensions, and Practice'. *Review of Research in Education*, 19, 3–49.

— (2006) 'Teaching Black History with a focus on decision-making'. In Banks, J.A. (ed.) *Race, Culture, and Education: The selected works of James A. Banks.* London and New York: Routledge.

Baptist, E.E. (2014) *The Half Has Never Been Told: Slavery and the making of American capitalism.* New York: Basic Books.

Barnett, R. (2008) 'Critical professionalism in an age of supercomplexity'. In Cunningham, B. (ed.) *Exploring Professionalism.* London: Institute of Education Publications.

Barton, K.C. (2009) 'The denial of desire: How to make history education meaningless'. In Symcox, L. and Wilschut, A. (eds) *National History Standards: The problem of the canon and the future of history teaching.* Charlotte, NC: IAP, 265–82.

Barton, K.C. and Levstik, L.S. (2004) *Teaching History for the Common Good.* Mahwah, NJ: Lawrence Erlbaum Associates.

BCA (Black Cultural Archives) (2014) Black Cultural Archives website. Online. http://bcaheritage.org.uk (accessed 10 July 2015).

Blackburn, R. (2010) *The Making of New World Slavery: From the Baroque to the Modern, 1492–1800.* London: Verso.

Blackmon, D. (2008). *Slavery by Another Name: The re-enslavement of Black people in America from the Civil War to World War II.* New York: Anchor.

Boffey, D. (2014) 'Only three black applicants win places to train as history teachers'. *The Guardian*, 22 March. Online. www.theguardian.com/education/2014/mar/22/black-graduate-history-teachers-institutional-racism (accessed 15 July 2015).

Brandt, G. (1986) *The Realization of Anti-Racist Teaching*. London: Falmer Press.

Brown, D. (1991) *Bury My Heart at Wounded Knee*. London: Vintage.

Brown, G. (2006) 'Fabian New Year Conference 2006: Who do we want to be?' Talk given at a conference on 'The future of Britishness', Imperial College, London, 14 January 2006. Online. www.fabians.org.uk/events/speeches/the-future-of-britishness (accessed 7 May 2012).

Burbules, N. (1993) *Dialogue in Teaching: Theory and practice*. New York: Teachers College Press.

Burnard, T. (2011) 'The Atlantic slave trade'. In Heuman, G. and Burnard, T. (eds) *The Routledge History of Slavery*. London and New York: Routledge.

Card, J. (2004) 'Seeing double: How one period visualises another'. *Teaching History*, 117, 6–11.

Carmichael, S. (2004) *Ready for Revolution: The life and struggles of Stokely Carmichael (Kwame Ture)*. New York: Scribner Press.

Carretta, V. and Reese, T.M. (2010) *The Life and Letters of Philip Quaque, The First African Anglican Missionary*. Athens: University of Georgia Press.

Carson, C. (2005) 'The unfinished dialogue of Martin Luther King Jr. and Malcolm X'. *Organization of American Historians*, 19 (1), 22–6.

Casciani, D. (2002) 'Troubled history of stop and search'. *BBC News*, 7 November. Online. http://news.bbc.co.uk/1/hi/uk/2246331.stm (accessed 25 August 2015).

Césaire, A. (1992) *A Tempest*. New York: Ubu Repertory Theater Publications.

CivilRightsVeterans.org (n.d.) 'Mississippi Freedom Summer Events. McComb: Breaking the Klan siege'. Online. www.crmvet.org/tim/tim64b.htm#1964mccomb (accessed 9 June 2015).

Clark Hine, D. (1994) *Hine Sight: Black women and the reconstruction of American history*. New York: Carlson Publishing.

Cone, J. (1992) *Martin & Malcolm & America: A dream or a nightmare*. Maryknoll, NY: Orbis Books.

Conway, R. (2006) 'What they think they know: The impact of pupils' preconceptions on their understanding of historical significance'. *Teaching History*, 125, 10–15.

Counsell, C. (2004) 'Looking through a Josephine-Butler-shaped window: Focusing pupils' thinking on historical significance'. *Teaching History*, 114, 30–6.

Cremin, H. and Warwick, P. (2008) 'Multiculturalism is dead: Long live community cohesion? A case study of an educational methodology to empower young people as global citizens'. *Research in Comparative and International Education*, 3 (1), 36–49.

Crosby, E.J. (2002) '"This nonviolent stuff ain't no good. It'll get ya killed.": Teaching about self-defense in the African American freedom struggle'. In Armstrong, J.B., Edwards, S.H., Roberson, H.B. and Williams, R.Y. (eds) *Teaching the American Civil Rights Movement: Freedom's bittersweet song*. New York: Routledge.

Daly, R.J. (1983) 'Samuel Pepys and post-traumatic stress disorder'. *British Journal of Psychiatry*, 143, 64–8.

Davidson, B. (1992) *The Black Man's Burden*. London: James Currey.

— (1994) *The Search for Africa: A history in the making*. London: James Currey.

Davies, C.B. (2008) *Left of Karl Marx: The political life of Black Communist Claudia Jones*. Durham, NC: Duke University Press.

Department for Education (DfE) (2013) 'National Curriculum in England: Citizenship programmes of study for key Stages 3 and 4'. London: DfE. Online. www.gov.uk/government/publications/national-curriculum-in-england-citizenship-programmes-of-study (accessed 4 August 2015).

— (2014) 'Promoting fundamental British values as part of SMSC in schools: Departmental advice for maintained schools'. London: DfE. Online. www.gov.uk/government/uploads/system/uploads/attachment_data/file/380595/SMSC_Guidance_Maintained_Schools.pdf (accessed 5th January 2016)

Department for Education and Science (1991) *The National Curriculum for History*. London: HMSO.

Dewey, J. (1933) *How We Think*. Boston and London: D.C. Heath.

Dictionary.com (n.d.) 'Troika'. Online. http://dictionary.reference.com/browse/troika (accessed 26 August 2015).

Diop, C.A. (1964) 'Evolution of the Negro world'. *Présence Africaine*, 23 (51), 5–15.

Dismantling the Master's House (2015) 'Dismantling the Master's House'. Online. www.dtmh.ucl.ac.uk (accessed 25 August 2015).

Dubow, S. (2007) 'Thoughts on South Africa: Some preliminary ideas'. In Stolten, H.E. (ed.) *History Making and Present Day Politics: The meaning of collective memory in South Africa*. Uppsala: Nordiska Afrikainstitutet.

— (2014) *Apartheid 1948–94*. Oxford: Oxford University Press.

Duncan-Andrade, J. (2009) 'Note to educators: Hope required when growing roses in concrete'. *Harvard Educational Review*, 79 (2), 181–94.

Dyson, M.E. (2000) *I May Not Get There With You: The true Martin Luther King, Jr.* New York: Free Press.

Education Week (2015) 'Quality Counts 2015: State report cards map'. Online. www.edweek.org/ew/qc/2015/2015-state-report-cards-map.html?intc=EW-QC15-LFTNAV (accessed 9 June 2015).

Epstein, T. (2009) *Interpreting National History: Race, identity, and pedagogy in classrooms and communities*. New York and London: Routledge.

Estes, S. (2005) *I am a Man! Race, manhood, and the Civil Rights Movement*. Chapel Hill: University of North Carolina Press.

Estlund, D. (2003) 'Why not epistocracy?' In Reshotko, N. (ed.) *Desire, Identity and Existence: Essays in honor of T.M. Penner*. Kelowna, BC: Academic Printing and Publishing.

Face to Face (1961) John Freeman's television interview with Martin Luther King, repeated on BBC 4, 5 August 2002.

Fairclough, A. (2001) *A Better Day Coming: Blacks and equality, 1890–2000*. New York and London: Viking.

Fei, L. (2007) 'A call for freedom: Aimé Césaire's "A Tempest"'. *Canadian Social Science*, 3 (5), 118–20.

Ferguson, N. (2003) *Empire: How Britain Made the Modern World*. London: Allen Lane.

Ford, J.C. and Bobb, K. (2011) 'Defending self worth: A hidden talent of children of the African diaspora'. In Freeman, K. and Johnson, E. (eds) *Education in the Black Diaspora*. New York and London: Routledge.

Forman, J. (1997) *The Making of Black Revolutionaries*. Seattle: University of Washington Press.

Fredrickson, G.M. (2002) *Racism: A short history*. Princeton: Princeton University Press.

Fryer, P. (1985) *Staying Power: The history of Black people in Britain*. London: Pluto Press.

Gardham, D. (2015) 'Inside the British battle to wipe out the scourge of Somali pirates: Not one hijacking has taken place in last two years in the Indian Ocean after 126 pirates were jailed'. *Daily Mail*, 13 February. Online. www.dailymail. co.uk/news/article-2950837/Inside-British-battle-wipe-scurge-Somali-pirates-Not-one-hijacking-taken-place-two-years-Indian-Ocean-126-pirates-jailed. html (accessed 25 August 2015).

Garrow, D.J. (1987) 'Martin Luther King, Jr. and the spirit of leadership'. *Journal of American History*, 74 (2), 438–47.

Giddings, P. (2007) *Where and When I Enter: The impact of Black women on race and sex in America*. New York: HarperCollins.

Giliomee, H. (2012) *The Last Afrikaner Leaders: A supreme test of power*. Cape Town: Tafelberg.

Gilroy, P. (1992) *There Ain't No Black in the Union Jack*. London: Routledge.

— (2007) *Black Britain: A photographic history*. London: SAQI.

Gove, M. (2011) 'National curriculum review: Children failed by Labour's education reforms, says Gove'. *Daily Telegraph*, 20 January.

Grant, C.A. (2011) 'Escaping Devil's Island: Confronting racism, learning history'. *Race, Ethnicity and Education*, 14 (1), 33–49.

Grant, S.G. and Gradwell, J.M. (2010) *Teaching History with Big Ideas: Cases of ambitious teachers*. Lanham, MD: Rowman and Littlefield.

Grosvenor, I. (1999) 'History and the perils of multiculturalism in 1990s Britain'. *Teaching History*, 97, 37–40.

Hall, S. (1999) 'From Scarman to Stephen Lawrence'. *History Workshop Journal*, 48, 187–97.

Halpin, D. (2003) *Hope and Education: The role of the utopian imagination*. London: RoutledgeFalmer.

Haq, H. (2014) 'Liberals and conservatives both object to new Texas textbooks'. *Christian Science Monitor*, 18 September. Online. www.csmonitor.com/Books/chapter-and-verse/2014/0918/Liberals-and-conservatives-both-object-to-new-Texas-textbooks (accessed 9 June 2015).

Harper, M. (2012) *Getting Somalia Wrong? Faith, war and hope in a shattered state*. London and New York: Zed Books.

Harris, H. (2004) *The Somali Community in the UK: What we know and how we know it*. London: The Information Centre about Asylum and Refugees in the UK (ICAR).

Hart, S., Dixon, A., Drummond, M.J. and McIntyre, D. (2004) *Learning without Limits*. Maidenhead: Open University Press.

References

Heitin, L. (2015) 'Rewrite of AP framework for U.S. history criticized'. *Education Week*, 3 March. Online. www.edweek.org/ew/articles/2015/03/04/objections-spread-to-ap-us-history-rewrite.html (accessed 9 June 2015).

Hinds, D. (2008) 'The West Indian Gazette: Claudia Jones and the black press in Britain'. *Race & Class*, 50 (1), 88–97.

Hirsch, Jr., E.D. (1988) *Cultural Literacy: What every American needs to know*. New York: Vintage Books.

Historical Thinking Matters (n.d.) 'Historical Thinking Matters'. Online. http://historicalthinkingmatters.org (accessed 9 June 2015).

Holsey, B. (2008) *Routes of Remembrance: Refashioning the slave trade in Ghana*. Chicago: University of Chicago Press.

Holt, T.C. (1992) *The Problem of Freedom: Race, labor, and politics in Jamaica and Britain, 1832–1938*. Baltimore: Johns Hopkins University Press.

— (1995) 'Marking: Race, race-making, and the writing of history'. *American Historical Review*, 100 (1), 1–20.

Horne, G. (2014) *The Counter-revolution of 1776: Slave resistance and the origins of the United States of America*. New York: New York University Press.

Howard, G.R. (2006) *We Can't Teach What We Don't Know: White teachers, multiracial schools*. New York and London: Teachers College Press.

Howe, D. (2004) 'Turning on each other'. *The Guardian*, 7 August. Online. www.theguardian.com/world/2004/aug/07/race.immigrationandpublicservices (accessed 30 July 2015).

Hughes, D., Smith, E.P., Johnson, D.J., Stevenson, H.C. and Spicer, P. (2006) 'Parents' ethnic-racial socialization practices: A review of research and directions for future study'. *Developmental Psychology*, 42 (5), 747–70.

Hull, A., Bell-Scott, P. and Smith, B. (1982) *But Some of Us Are Brave: All the women are white, all the Blacks are men: Black women's studies*. New York: Feminist Press.

In Our Time (1999) 'Africa', with Melvyn Bragg (BBC Radio 4, 9 July 1999) [radio programme]. Online. www.bbc.co.uk/programmes/p00545ld (accessed 27 July 2015).

Jensen, R. (2005) *The Heart of Whiteness: Confronting race, racism, and white privilege*. San Francisco: City Lights.

Jones, J. (2013) *A Dreadful Deceit: The myth of race from the colonial era to Obama's America*. New York: Basic Books.

Jordan, G. (2004) *Somali Elders: Portraits from Wales / Odeyada Soomaalida: Muuqaalo Ka Yimid Welishka*. Cardiff: Butetown History and Arts Centre.

Kahin, M. (1997) *Educating Somali Children in Britain*. Stoke on Trent: Trentham Books.

Kaufmann, M. (2014) 'Blanke, John (fl. 1507–1512)'. In Goldman, L. (ed.) *Oxford Dictionary of National Biography*. Oxford: Oxford University Press.

Kelly, E.B. (1968) 'Murder of the American Dream'. *College Composition and Communication*, 19 (2), 106–8.

Khan, H., McPhee, M. and Goldman, R. (2009) 'Obama called police officer who arrested Gates, still sees "overreaction" in arrest'. *ABC News*, 24 July. Online. http://abcnews.go.com/Politics/story?id=8163051&page=1 (accessed 5 July 2015).

Kierkegaard, S. (1992) *Either/Or: A fragment of life*. London: Penguin Classics.

King, M.L. (1958) *Stride toward Freedom: The Montgomery story*. New York: Harper & Row.

Kitson, A., Husbands, C. and Steward, C. (2011) *Teaching and Learning History 11–18: Understanding the past*. Maidenhead: Open University Press.

Ladson-Billings, G. (1995) 'Toward a theory of culturally relevant pedagogy'. *American Education Research Journal*, 32 (3), 465–91.

Lamont Hill, M. (2009) *Beats, Rhymes, and Classroom Life: Hip-hop pedagogy and the politics of identity*. New York: Teachers College Press.

Landsman, J.G. and Lewis, C.W. (eds) (2011) *White Teachers / Diverse Classrooms: Creating inclusive schools, building on students' diversity and providing true educational equality*. Sterling, VA: Stylus Publishing.

Lee, E., Menkart, D. and Okazawa-Rey, M. (1998) *Beyond Heroes and Holidays: A practical guide to K–12 multicultural, anti-racist education and staff development*. Washington, DC: Teaching for Change.

Lee, P. and Shemilt, D. (2004) '"I just wish we could go back in the past and find out what really happened": Progression in understanding about historical accounts'. *Teaching History*, 117, 25–31.

Lerner, A. (2015) 'History class becomes a debate on America'. *Politico*, 21 February. Online. www.politico.com/story/2015/02/ap-us-history-controversy-becomes-a-debate-on-america-115381.html (accessed 9 June 2015).

Lorde, A. (2007) 'The master's tools will never dismantle the master's house'. In Lorde, A. (ed.) *Sister Outsider: Essays and speeches*. Berkeley, CA: Crossing Press.

The Lost Libraries of Timbuktu (2009), television documentary written and presented by Aminatta Forna, produced by Richard Trayler-Smith (BBC 4, 12 February).

Lyndon, D. (2006) 'Integrating Black British history into the National Curriculum'. *Teaching History*, 122, 37–43.

Ma, X. (2003) 'Sense of belonging to school: Can schools make a difference?' *Journal of Educational Research*, 96 (6), 340–9.

Macpherson, S.W. (1999) *The Stephen Lawrence Inquiry: Report of an inquiry*. London: The Stationery Office.

Mandela, N. (1990) 'The struggle is my life'. BBC World Service. Online. www.bbc.co.uk/worldservice/specials/1246_land/page8.shtml (accessed 5 December 2015).

Marable, M. (1991) *Race, Reform, and Rebellion: The second Reconstruction in black America, 1945–1990*. Jackson: University Press of Mississippi.

— (2006) *Living Black History*. New York: Basic/Civitas Books.

Margaret Thatcher Foundation (n.d.) 'TV Interview for Granada World in Action ("rather swamped")'. Online. www.margaretthatcher.org/document/103485 (accessed 25 August 2015).

Maton, K. (2014) 'Habitus'. In Grenfell, M. (ed.) *Pierre Bourdieu: Key concepts*. Abingdon: Routledge.

Maylor, U. (2010) 'Notions of diversity, British identities and citizenship belonging'. *Race, Ethnicity and Education*, 13 (2), 233–52.

McComb Legacies (2011) About McComb Legacies. Online. http://mccomblegacies.org/about (accessed 9 June 2015).

References

Menkart, D., Murray, A.D. and View, J. (2004). *Putting the Movement Back into Civil Rights Teaching: A resource guide for classrooms and communities.* Washington, DC: Poverty and Race Research Action Council and Teaching for Change.

Meredith, M. (2011) *Born in Africa: The quest for the origins of human life.* New York: PublicAffairs.

Mississippi Truth Project (n.d.) 'Teaching Civil Rights History in Mississippi'. Online. www.mississippitruth.org/pages/CR-education.htm (accessed 9 June 2015).

Mohamud, A. and Whitburn, R. (2014) 'Unpacking the suitcase and finding history: Doing justice to the teaching of diverse histories in the classroom'. *Teaching History,* 154, 40–6.

Montaigne, M. de (2004) *The Essays: A selection.* London: Penguin.

Morgan, P.D. (2004) 'The Black experience in the British Empire, 1680–1810'. In Morgan, P.D. and Hawkins, S. (eds) *Black Experience and the Empire.* Oxford: Oxford University Press.

Mosely, K. (2008) 'Vote for hope'. *Pittsburgh Post-Gazette,* 2 November. Online. www.post-gazette.com/Op-Ed/2008/11/02/Vote-for-hope/stories/200811020185 (accessed 9 June 2015).

Mullard, C. (1973) *Black Britain.* London: Allen and Unwin.

New Policy Institute (1998) *Second Chances: Exclusion from school and equality of opportunity.* London: New Policy Institute.

Obama, B. (2006) *The Audacity of Hope.* New York: Random House.

Olusoga, D. (2014) *The World's War.* London: Head of Zeus.

Onyeka (2013) *Blackamoores: Africans in Tudor England, their presence, status and origins.* London: Narrative Eye.

Operation Black Vote (2013) 'We've won! Mary Seacole, Olaudah Equiano'. Online. www.obv.org.uk/news-blogs/we-ve-won-mary-seacole-olaudah-equiano (accessed 15 July 2015).

Osler, A. (2009) 'Patriotism, multiculturalism and belonging: Political discourse and the teaching of history'. *Educational Review,* 61 (1), 85–100.

Palos, A.L. and McGinnis, E.I. (2012) 'Precious Knowledge'. Online. http://itvs.org/films/precious-knowledge (accessed 9 June 2015).

Pankhania, J. (1994) *Liberating the National History Curriculum.* London: Falmer.

Pankhurst, R. (1977) 'An early Somali autobiography (II)'. *Africa,* 32 (3), 355–83.

Pogrund, B. (2006) *How Can Man Die Better? The life of Robert Sobukwe.* Johannesburg and Cape Town: Jonathan Ball.

Powell, Enoch (1968) 'Rivers of Blood' speech. Full text online. www.telegraph.co.uk/comment/3643823/Enoch-Powells-Rivers-of-Blood-speech.html

Prozesky, M. (2009) 'Cinderella, survivor and saviour: African ethics and the quest for a global ethic'. In Murove, M.F. (ed.) *African Ethics: An anthology of comparative and applied ethics.* Scottsville: University of KwaZulu Natal Press.

QCA (Qualifications and Curriculum Authority) (2007) 'History programme of study for Key Stage 3 and attainment target'. London: Department for Education.

Racism: A history (2007) television documentary series produced by David Okuefuna, BBC 4, March.

Ramdin, R. (1999) *Reimaging Britain: 500 years of Black and Asian history.* London: Pluto Press.

Rasmussen, J. (2011) 'Education for Somali students in London: Challenges and strategies'. *Macalester Abroad: Research and writing from off-campus study*, 3 (1). Online. http://digitalcommons.macalester.edu/macabroad/vol3/iss1/4 (accessed 30 July 2015).

Riley, M. (2000) 'Into the Key Stage 3 history garden: Choosing and planting your history questions'. *Teaching History*, 99, 8–13.

Rousseau, J-J. (1979) *Emile, or On Education.* Trans. and ed. Bloom, A. New York: Basic Books.

Saad, E. (2010) *Social History of Timbuktu: The role of Muslim scholars and notables, 1400–1900.* Cambridge: Cambridge University Press.

Sandbrook, D. (2005) *Never Had It So Good: A history of Britain from Suez to the Beatles.* London: Abacus.

Saxton, A. (1990) *The Rise and Fall of the White Republic: Class politics and mass culture in nineteenth-century America.* London: Verso.

Seal, A. and Bailey, R. (2013) 'The 2011 famine in Somalia: Lessons learnt from a failed response?' *Conflict and Health*, 7 (22). http://doi.org/10.1186/1752-1505-7-22 (accessed 5 January 2016).

Seixas, P. and Morton, T. (2013) *The Big Six Historical Thinking Concepts.* Toronto: Nelson/Cengage Learning.

Semmel, B. (1962) 'The issue of "race" in the British reaction to the Morant Bay Uprising of 1865'. *Caribbean Studies*, 2 (3), 3–15.

Sen, A. (2010) *The Idea of Justice.* London and New Delhi: Penguin Books.

Sherwood, M. (1999) *Claudia Jones: A life in exile.* London: Lawrence and Wishart.

Smith, N. (1992) *Black Peoples of the Americas*, Oxford: Oxford University Press.

Smith, Steven R. (1977) '"Decidedly Different": The Seventeenth Century and Africa'. *History Today*, 27 (1), 41.

Southern Poverty Law Center (2014) *Teaching the Movement: The state of civil rights education in the United States, 2014.* Report by the Southern Poverty Law Center's Teaching Tolerance Program, Montgomery, Alabama. Online. www.tolerance.org/sites/default/files/general/Teaching%20the%20 Movement%202014_final_web_0.pdf (accessed 9 June 2015).

Starkey, D. (2011) 'England riots: "The whites have become black"'. *Newsnight* interview, 13 August. Online. www.bbc.co.uk/news/uk-14513517 (accessed 3 December 2015).

Stevens, S. (2012) 'A grand design'. *Diplomatic History*, 36 (5), 797–800.

Stolten, H.E. (2007) 'History in the new South Africa: An introduction'. In Stolten, H.E. (ed.) *History Making and Present Day Politics: The meaning of collective memory in South Africa.* Uppsala: Nordiska Afrikainstitutet.

Strand, S. (2007) *Minority Ethnic Pupils in the Longitudinal Study of Young People in England (LSYPE).* Nottingham: Department for Children, Schools and Families.

Street, J. (2008) 'Malcolm X, Smethwick, and the influence of the African American freedom struggle on British race relations in the 1960s'. *Journal of Black Studies*, 38 (6), 932–50.

References

Sugrue, T.J. (2010) *Not Even Past: Barack Obama and the burden of race.* Princeton: Princeton University Press.

Sutherland, M. (2006) 'African Caribbean immigrants in the United Kingdom: The legacy of racial disadvantages'. *Caribbean Quarterly,* 52 (1), 26–52.

Swalwell, K., Pellegrino, A.M. and View, J.L. (2014) 'Teachers' curricular choices when teaching histories of oppressed people: Capturing the U.S. Civil Rights Movement'. *Journal of Social Studies Research,* 39 (2), 79–94.

TeachingHistory.org (n.d.) 'Historical Thinking'. Online. http://teachinghistory.org/historical-thinking-intro (accessed 9 June 2015).

Tegeler, P. (2013) 'Diverse classrooms also benefit white children'. *Huffington Post,* 3 January. Online. www.huffingtonpost.com/philip-tegeler/diverse-classrooms-also-b_b_2403328.html (accessed 3 December 2015).

Theoharis, J. (2009) '"A life history of being rebellious": The radicalism of Rosa Parks'. In Gore, D.F., Theoharis, J. and Woodard, K. (eds) *Want to Start a Revolution? Radical women in the Black freedom struggle.* New York: New York University Press.

Traille, K. (2007) '"You should be proud about your history. They made me feel ashamed": Teaching history hurts'. *Teaching History,* 127, 31–7.

Tyson, T.B. (1999) *Radio Free Dixie: Robert F. Williams and the roots of Black Power.* Chapel Hill: University of North Carolina Press.

United Nations General Assembly (2014) 'Resolution adopted by the General Assembly on 18 November 2014: 69/16. Programme of activities for the implementation of the International Decade for People of African Descent'. Online. www.un.org/en/events/africandescentdecade/pdf/A.RES.69.16_IDPAD.pdf (accessed 24 August 2015).

US Supreme Court (1896) *Plessy vs. Ferguson,* Judgement, Decided 18 May 1896; Records of the Supreme Court of the United States; Record Group 267; *Plessy v. Ferguson,* 163, #15248. Washington, D.C.: National Archives. Online. www.ourdocuments.gov/doc.php?doc=52

Verney, K. (2006) *The Debate on Black Civil Rights in America.* Manchester: Manchester University Press.

View, J.L. (2013) '"I was and am": Historical counternarrative as nonviolent resistance in the United States'. In Amster, R. and Ndura, E. (eds) *Exploring the Power of Nonviolence: Peace, politics and practice.* Syracuse, NY: Syracuse University Press.

Walvin. J. (2000) *Making the Black Atlantic: Britain and the African diaspora.* London: Cassell.

Waters, R. (2013) 'Black Power on the telly: Re-thinking re-racialisation in Britain'. Paper presented at the Institute of Commonwealth Studies, London, 7 June.

Whitaker, B. (2004) 'Kilroy-Silk investigated for anti-Arab comments'. *The Guardian,* 8 January. Online. www.theguardian.com/media/2004/jan/08/pressandpublishing.raceintheuk (accessed 23 August 2015).

Whitburn, R. and Yemoh, S. (2012) '"My people struggled too": Hidden histories and heroism – a school-designed, post-14 course on multi-cultural Britain since 1945'. *Teaching History,* 147, 16–25.

Whitburn, R., Hussain, M. and Mohamud, A. (2012) '"Doing justice to history": The learning of African history in a North London secondary school and teacher development in the spirit of Ubuntu'. *Teaching History,* 146, 18–27.

Whitman, W. (2015) 'Myself and mine'. In Whitman, W. *Leaves of Grass*. Tustin, CA: Xist Publishing.

Who You Callin' a Nigger? (2004), television documentary presented by Darcus Howe, Channel 4, 9 August.

Wilkinson, M.L.N. (2014) 'The concept of the absent curriculum: The case of the Muslim contribution and the English National Curriculum for history'. *Journal of Curriculum Studies*, 46 (4), 419–40.

Williams, R.F. (2013) *Negroes With Guns*. Mansfield Center, CT: Martino Publishing.

Willinsky, J. (1998) *Learning to Divide the World*. Minneapolis: University of Minnesota Press.

Wineburg, S. (2001) *Historical Thinking and Other Unnatural Acts*. Philadelphia: Temple University Press.

Wineburg, S. and Monte-Sano, C. (2008) '"Famous Americans": The changing pantheon of American heroes'. *Journal of American History,* 94 (4), 1186–1202.

W.K. Kellogg Foundation (2015) 'Grants: Teaching for Change'. Online. www.wkkf.org/grants/grant/2011/06/a-community-of-promise-building-strong-schools-and-neighborhoods-through-history-activism-and-collab (accessed 9 June 2015).

Woodson, C.G. (2009) *The Miseducation of the Negro*. New York: Classic Books.

World Heritage Encyclopedia (2015) 'List of U.S. states by African American population'. In *World Heritage Encyclopedia*. Online. www.worldheritage.org/article/WHEBN0020010164/List%20of%20U.S.%20states%20by%20African American%20population (accessed 9 June 2015).

Index

Index